Published in Australia by Corvus Publishing
Street: 4/1 Violet St ESSENDON, 3040
Email: dcorbett@westnet.com.au
Website: dcorbett.com.au

First published in Australia 2010
Copyright © David A Corbett 2010
Cover design: John Lowe
Typesetting: Felicity Gilbert

National Library of Australia Cataloguing-in-Publication entry
Author: Corbett, David A. (David Albert), 1940- author.
Title: The lies of the land : a guide to our corrupt society / David A Corbett.
ISBN: 9780992414405 (paperback)
Notes: Includes index.

Subjects: Political ethics.
Political corruption.
Social ethics.
Good and evil.

Dewey Number: 172

The Lies of the Land

A guide to our corrupt society

―――――――――

Dr David A Corbett

ABOUT | THE AUTHOR

David Corbett graduated in Medicine from Melbourne University in 1964. He subsequently trained as a specialist Anaesthetist. He has spent one year in the United States, one year in Saudi Arabia and many years in city and rural hospitals in Australia in that specialty.

He has also gained qualifications in accounting, finance and investment and has a diploma from the Institute of Company Directors. He has a continued interest in mathematics and physics as well as studying Electronic engineering for four years part time. He was also a Councillor on the Essendon City Council for three years.

PRE|FACE

Our world is manipulated by those in power. The goals of political intrigue are rarely those in the interests of humanity but commonly in the commercial interests of the rulers. The main weapon of our rulers is fear. Once fear is instilled, their motives are not then questioned.

The history we are taught about World War II does not bear any logical scrutiny. There is bountiful evidence to suggest that Hitler and the Western powers had covert agreements and co-ordinated actions. An examination of the Nuremberg trials leads to the inexorable conclusion that they had nothing to do with justice and everything to do with the extermination of witnesses to a criminal conspiracy.

Regrettably, deceit is not limited to politicians. Virtually every special group in society practices some form of misrepresentation to protect its own powers and the prestige of its members. These misrepresentations ultimately cost us all dearly. But there is also a cost to the perpetrators: their own advancement is stalled because their self-serving propaganda blinds them to greater truths.

We thus have corruption in science and education. We have prisons whose costs far outweigh their benefits. We have climate-change doomsayers instilling irrational fear in others in order to convince themselves that they are saving humanity from itself.

In short, instilled fear paralyses our powers of logic to the point that we readily accept political actions that would otherwise be regarded as patently absurd.

Our rulers maintain their position by telling us what they want us to believe. These lies – the Lies of the Land – are used to keep people in fear and thereby protect the rulers from displacement.

All classes of society perpetuate myths to maintain the control of their senior members.

This book is aimed at exposing many such lies, and suggests ways of detecting and resisting them.

CONT|ENTS

INTRO|DUCTION

In his novel, *Candide*, Voltaire maintained that we presently live in the best of all possible worlds – under the circumstances. Now, a cursory look around us tells us that all is not well in the state of Denmark. We have wars, famine, fire and floods; we have obscene wealth living cheek by jowl with abject poverty; we have young folk wasting or destroying their lives with drugs in back alleys, or in cars on our roads.

Why then is our world only the best possible and not the ideal? To answer this question, we need to appreciate what is really going on in our world and to understand how we got to our present state. But what is the ideal world? What do we really want? The only undeniable purpose of our existence is that of procreation. The rest of our time on earth is only of use to us if we use it to achieve things which give us pleasure or to fulfil other personal goals.

For fulfilment and happiness, we need to be free to pursue our personal ambitions. Commonly, such goals involve contributions of benefit to society. Happiness only occurs during the pursuit or achievement of goals — the anticipation usually exceeding the consummation. When people no longer have any purpose in living, they are quite content to die. Contrariwise, even terminally ill people tend to hold on until they have had the opportunity to say goodbye to loved ones or to see the achievement of some personal objective.

Although our civilisation consists of a myriad of individuals, each person is unique with individual talents. Mostly, these talents go unrecognised and unused. Surely, we are grateful for the range of facilities available to us – cars, washing machines, etc., but how many inventors in our community will live and die with talents that remain undeveloped and contributions unsung? If each individual was allowed and encouraged to achieve his or her best, our society would be much richer and civilisation would progress much more rapidly than it presently does. Would any of us suffer detriment if we encouraged all of the world's talents to be expressed rather than stifling a large proportion? Contributions to society are not an even-sum game wherein a contribution by one person would deny another person the privilege of also contributing.

What does an individual require in order to derive the greatest happiness and fulfilment in life? In my view:

1. Every individual must be allowed and encouraged to pursue their goals.

2. Everyone must be free to make their own choices. And if each and every individual is to be free, it follows that no individual should infringe the freedom of another.

3. Every person will achieve a greater potential if they are assisted in their endeavours by others. As each individual will contribute the most to society if they are allowed to reach their full potential, it follows that

it is in everyone's interests to help others rather than oppose them.

The above points bring us to the subject of selfishness. Our minds and bodies are dedicated to our own personal survival and fulfilment. Selfishness is not a crime and it is important to our own well-being and achievement. Ultimate selfishness is exclusively looking to one's own advantage. With experience, we learn to plan ahead and we also learn that selfishness is best served by enlisting the help of others. The price of that help is that we must usually return the favour. It follows, then, that selfishness is not necessarily detrimental to others if it is also advantageous to them as well as to ourselves.

Co-operative objectives were presumably adhered to in primitive societies. Why then has our society veered away from these principles? The answer, I believe, resides in the third point above — in order to expand our personal successes it is much easier if we enlist help. Those who achieve positions of power initially enlist help but ultimately transform themselves to a position wherein they dictate to others. This transition commonly involves the use of lies and deceit. Lies and deceit avoid the problem of honestly convincing others that the ruler has some inherent right to privilege.

From childhood, we are taught many false ideas. Some people are advantaged by this deception, but society as a whole and the average person in particular, is disadvantaged. The progress of science and human relations are also stultified as a result. We have carnage and human suffering that is totally unnecessary. There is enough food in this world to feed its entire population but the denial of resources as a result of political greed leads to regions of mass starvation.

Lies and deceits may be ultimately uncovered and ignored. However, when fear is added to the mix, even obvious lies become treated with some respect on the basis that it may be unsafe to ignore them.

There are some whimsical concepts that serve for pleasure and joy in childhood. Although we later find them to be erroneous, we accept them as harmless concepts that make our world a richer place in which to live. On the other hand, there are other concepts we have been taught to accept as true but later find to be not common practice at all. We were taught that adultery is immoral — but later learn that about 80% of married folk indulge in it at least once in their lives. Maybe if nobody committed adultery, our society might be better, but how can we ever prove that? We were also taught not to kill — but we find that nations do it on a wholesale basis. State murder (war) is acceptable but personal murder is not. Why?

Those in power use fear to maintain control. Ideally, the fear is of some event that might occur in the future as this cannot be disproven at the present time. It is said that 80% of our fears about the future never come to pass. In engendering and maintaining fear, our rulers usually need to bypass logic. This is never a problem because once emotion is introduced, logic is discarded. We therefore have situations where we pigeon-hole ideas — we can accept a total lack of logic in one situation, but we would ridicule the same logic if it were applied to another, more familiar situation.

To sustain fear, the authorities must resort to lies and deception — *The Lies of the Land.* The imposition of rules and laws is presented to us as something for our protection and benefit. There is some logic in this, but we need to realise that the purpose of laws promulgated by our rulers is, first and foremost, for the benefit of those rulers themselves, and any benefit we derive from those laws is really an unintended consequence.

Oft times, we lose sight of the arbitrary nature of rules and customs and tend to believe that certain actions are inherently right or wrong because that is what we have been brought up to believe. Consequently, our training is a two-edged sword: on the one hand, we need to have a certain degree of conformity to prevent chaos in our society, but on the other hand, some rules only serve to benefit those who wish to rule us.

The confusion and lack of appreciation of the basis of our rules and laws leads us to accept much of what we were told without question or debate. One result is that we betray and short-sell our children by failing to explain to them the reasons underpinning certain civilised niceties. We simply instruct our young ones that certain things are right or wrong. Niceties, such as courtesy thus become regarded as authoritarian burdens which no self-respecting child could be expected to accept without rebellion. Our children are taught to tell the truth—but 'white lies' are okay; adultery is wrong, but everyone does it; murder is wrong, but war is glorious. Our children and hence our future adults, thereby enter a world that accepts hypocrisy as the norm.

Greed, lies, and deception are not the monopoly of any one societal group. We find the same characteristics in virtually all disciplines. Education, health, research, churches, and even charities exhibit a fair share of deceit.

The polarisation of society into rulers and the oppressed is a disadvantage to us by stifling the contributions that so many could make if only they had the opportunity. Even the rulers would benefit from an increased freedom and encouragement of the masses.

It is only when we begin to understand the causes of deceit and oppression that these evils can be countered. And it is only by opposing these harms that the people of this world will have any chance of living in harmony and enjoying the fruits of progress to which, in my view, we are all entitled.

The fact that we are deceived is understandable,

but the inability to understand our own lives is also an obstacle for us. If we don't see our goals clearly, we are likely to continue on a purposeless path simply because we know no other way.

'If you don't know where you are going, any road will take you there'
Lewis Carroll (1832-1898)

The aim of this book, then, is to:

1. understand how hierarchies develop;

2. understand how our rulers use psychological pressures to manipulate others to serve their own interests;

3. observe some of our institutions and how they are corrupted by our rulers;

4. examine how violence and wars are used to profit those in exalted positions and examine some global concerns and how they are used as a basis for political manipulation.

PART I

DEVELOPMENT OF HIERARCHIES

1 | THE COURSE OF LIFE

'One thing is certain and the rest is lies
The flower that once has blown, forever dies'
Omar Khayyam (1048-1131)

Let us consider what might be an ideal life and start from what we indisputably know to be true. We know that we are born, we develop through childhood to adulthood, we age and ultimately die. In the course of this progression, we have a drive to procreate. With procreation and a subsequent birth, the cycle repeats.

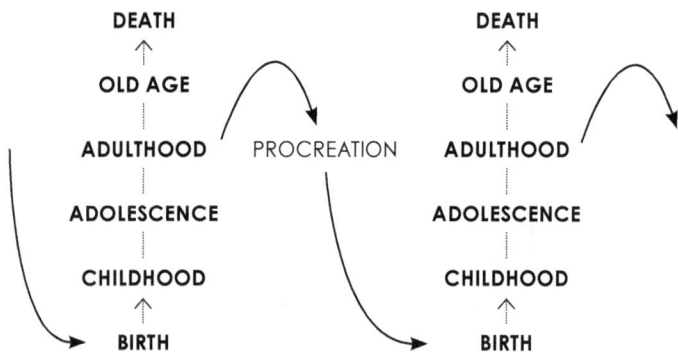

DEATH		DEATH
OLD AGE		OLD AGE
ADULTHOOD	PROCREATION	ADULTHOOD
ADOLESCENCE		ADOLESCENCE
CHILDHOOD		CHILDHOOD
BIRTH		BIRTH

The only indisputable reason for our existence is procreation. For all our pretensions at human importance, our lot, in the scheme of things, is no more exalted than that of a messenger-boy. We are simply here to carry germ-plasm from one generation to the next.

From nature's point of view, any individual is quite dispensable. Those who are the fittest and the most adaptable, survive — those who are not, die. Those who claim that humans have a 'right to life' have no evidence to support that contention and they can point to no power that enforces such a right. We all ultimately die. If we have a 'right to life', when did we receive it and at what point does it expire?

If the above progression is all there is to life (and we have no logical evidence to the contrary), we are left with an enormous amount of time to fill. In order to make the most of this time, we can only aim to derive as much pleasure and job satisfaction as possible. The things that give pleasure and satisfaction can only be determined by each individual themselves.

In order to pursue personal happiness, a person must be free to make his or her own choices. Thus, we can appreciate why men and women of all eras have fought and died for freedom. If every individual is to be free, it follows that no individual should be allowed to infringe the freedom of another. This would proscribe slavery and prevent any person from imposing his or her religious or political views on another. We therefore have to accept, without question, that each individual is entitled to their own ideas and actions providing that these do not interfere with the rights of anyone else.

'I am free to wave my arms about as much as I like, but my freedom ends where your nose begins.'

Anon

We may not agree with another person's point of view but, because there are no absolute standards with which everyone agrees, we are obliged to accept that an opposing point of view could possibly be just as correct as our own.

The importance of respecting the freedoms and ideas of others is that if I don't respect your rights, why should you respect mine? The denial of *anyone's* rights ultimately leads to the possible denial of *everyone's* rights. If, today, I can force you to act as I wish, there is a good chance that tomorrow you might be able to force me to act as you wish. Under these circumstances, we are all subject to interference and oppression and no-one can be sure of enjoying any freedom.

Taking this 'live and let live' concept a step further, we find that if we work together, we can achieve more than if we work alone. This does not mean that we need to sacrifice ourselves to a common good — a sacrifice is an imposition on the individual and therefore an infringement on his or her freedom. However, it does oblige us to consider the needs of others in any action we might take. We ultimately do ourselves a greater service by helping others rather than by obstructing them. Wouldn't we all achieve much more, and wouldn't our civilisation be much richer if we co-operated rather than competed with each other?

> *'Full many a bloom is born to blush unseen*
> *And waste its sweetness on the desert air.'*
> Thomas Gray (1716-1771)

If every individual was regarded as important in their own right, if no-one interfered with the lives of others and we all set out to help each other to achieve the best they can, what sort of society would we have? Would we have road-rage or theft or murder? Would we have wars, poverty or oppression of minorities? If everyone acted according to the above precepts, there would only remain one crime that required societal condemnation—the crime of *discourtesy*.

2 | SELF INTEREST

One of the many concepts in life that we tend not to question is that of selfishness or self-interest. It is not 'nice' to be selfish, so we ignore the practical importance of it and the integral part it plays in our lives.

Our bodies and minds are engineered to serve ourselves, not others. My heart, for example, is built to pump blood through my body not yours—although you are quite welcome to it when I am finished with it—my brain is engineered to look after my interests, not yours. The most important person in one's life is *oneself*. Because of this, totalitarian states never succeed in the long term. Even in totalitarian states, the police and military are kept on side by ensuring they receive special perks for their support of the rulers.

This emphasis on the importance of the individual does not mean that society will eventually become an anarchy consisting of a multitude of greedy individuals. Most people accept the advantages of collective action and co-operation to make their own lives more pleasant. However, in order to achieve our personal goals we must clearly understand that our own interests are paramount.

We have but one life and it is up to us to make the most of it. Fitting into the aspirations of others will not bring us satisfaction unless those aspirations also coincide with ours.

The reason we are taught not to be selfish is usually to coerce us into doing someone else's bidding; it is rarely in our own interests. It is a valuable exercise to examine the motivation of the person who accuses you of selfishness — what is *he* or *she* going to get out of it if you do as they say? And what are you going to get out of it if you take the course they are suggesting?

Selfishness is not sinful or antisocial because it is the engine of personal achievement. Many goals start and end as a simple pipe-dreams. Many teenagers dream of becoming singers or rock stars, but how many actually fulfil these dreams?

There are ways of achieving goals:

1. You must decide on the goal you wish to achieve. Ask yourself if the goal is the one that you personally want to achieve. Or, are you aspiring to a goal only because someone else has led you to believe that it is worthwhile. If it doesn't excite you personally, don't waste your life trying to achieve it.

2. You must determine the pathway to that objective. This involves planning a course of action.

   'Once you have decided to do something, the job is half done.'
   Abraham Lincoln (1809–1865)

3. Be prepared to accept the risks and the cost. If you want to become a doctor, that will require sacrifice of

many other pleasures and years of your time to study. Are you really prepared to make these sacrifices? Is the goal really worth it? There is no such thing as a free lunch, and when offered one you should carefully determine the ultimate price.

Our ship of life might be occasionally buffeted and taken off course by other events but we must keep our home-port clearly in mind through it all. There will always be some unavoidable detours so we must be flexible.

Greed is good insofar as it motivates us to take productive action. This does not mean that our greed should infringe upon the rights or progress of others, but we should not be ashamed of our own desires to acquire and accumulate. There are many examples where greed does cause grief and disadvantage to others, but a healthy respect for one's own advancement is not a crime.

If we are to have a harmonious society we must live and let live. We must accord to each person the right to their own beliefs and respect the sovereignty of each individual. This might seem like an unselfish exhortation. In reality, this consideration is ultimately one of self-interest. My freedom is only guaranteed if everyone's freedom is guaranteed and hence my interests are best served when I protect the interests of my neighbour.

'Conscience is that which makes us behave well when nobody is looking'

Anon

The above argument also applies to the consideration of animals. Without other creatures, our planet would be an unbearable place to live. We have the power to destroy animals but it is in our own interests to protect them. Animals presumably also have joys of life. Again, the concept comes down to self-interest: my environment will be much better if I also consider the welfare of animals.

We do not become members of a society for the benefit of society; we remain members of a society *for the benefits that the society confers upon us.* Where an individual is disadvantaged by a society, they tend to move to a society that provides them with the advantages they desire. This may mean moving to another country or to a different stratum of society (such as a criminal environment). Politicians never ask people to voluntarily pay more tax for the benefit of society — they always buy votes by promising to give us something. The fact that they are buying our votes with *our* money (i.e. we will inevitably pay more tax) probably never occurs to us.

We say we choose to live in a free society. What does that really mean?

There is no such thing as absolute freedom. We only choose the *types of freedoms* that we want, and accept the loss of other freedoms as a trade-off. I choose the freedoms which I get in a particular society. In return, I sacrifice my freedom to murder people and usurp any property I might desire.

It is very important to realise the limited nature of freedom. We are often exhorted by politicians to fight to defend freedom. But what freedoms are they talking about? The defence of freedom usually means the defence of our rulers' freedoms. When sent to war to 'defend freedom', it is wise to determine exactly what freedom we are fighting for. It is not inconceivable that the freedoms offered by the enemy might give us a better life than the one we presently have.

So when we talk of being 'free to pursue our goals', that freedom is always limited. If you and I are both to be optimally free, it follows that neither of us can be free to do anything which interferes with the freedom of the other. If that results in the other person acting in ways that we don't like personally, we have no right to interfere unless those actions interfere with the freedoms of others.

As there is no such thing as perfect freedom, we must decide what type of freedoms we want. Presently, there are a number of controversial issues in our society: *homosexuality*, *abortion*, and *euthanasia*. Attitudes towards these issues are based on the emotions of religious upbringing and not on any logic. People, of course, are entitled to their religious views and entitled to regulate their lives according to those views, but there is no reason why personal views should be forced on those who think otherwise.

Homosexuality

Providing a person's sexual preference does not interfere with any non-consensual person, by what logic does society make that preference to be illegal? We all seem to have an inherent antagonism to those who look or think differently, but before opposing a different point of view, we should ask ourselves whether we have the right to interfere in someone's life if they do not interfere with ours.

Abortion

My body is my possession. Nobody else can own my body. The law even asserts that no-one can own someone else's body (or corpse as the case might be). If my body is my sovereign possession, then nobody but me can deal with it. If I choose to allow my body to be used by someone else, surely that is my choice and my right. If I choose not to allow my body to be used by someone else, surely that is also my choice and my right.

Is this argument any less valid for a woman? If a woman chooses not to allow her body to be used for the creation of a child, that is her sovereign right. If she is pregnant, at what point does the unborn child assume a superior claim to her body? We seem to have a conflict of interest here — two individuals contesting the one body. Removal of the baby results in killing an unborn child. On the other hand, if the mother is prevented from terminating a pregnancy, she is being denied the sovereignty over her own body. It is a matter of deciding who is the 'a priori' owner of the body when such a conflict arises. Given that the unborn child cannot lead an independent existence outside the mother's body, then it surely does not have a prior right to require the mother to maintain it. If you are drowning, you have no *right* to my services in order to save you, nor do you have a *right* to a transfusion of my blood even though you might surely die without it.

Personally, I do not like the idea of abortion – it is destructive and wasteful. I have yet to meet a woman who had an abortion and does not have some degree of sadness about it. Many suffer a great deal of guilt. Most wonder about the potential of the child that might have been. Women do not usually have abortions by preference but due to circumstance. It may result from societal pressure for an unmarried woman not to have a child or it may be that the woman cannot afford to provide for the child. It is rarely because the woman would not have the child if circumstances were different.

Euthanasia

In respect to 'mercy killing', there are two quite distinct and separate issues:

1. Where a person wishes to terminate his or her own life. This is a matter of sovereignty in which the individual is dealing with their own property and not affecting anyone else.

2. Where a person wishes to terminate the life of another person who may not wish their life to be terminated.

If I come to the conclusion that there is no point for a person that is old and senile to continue to live, should I have the right to terminate that life? Clearly *not*, especially if I believe in not interfering with the sovereignty of another person.

But, what if a person is in constant pain due to an incurable disease and wishes to terminate his or her own life? In this case, anyone really believing in sovereignty of the individual must allow that person to die if that is their wish. As a doctor, I have had it put to me on more than one occasion: 'Doctor, if I were a dog, you would put me down. Why are you keeping me alive just to keep me suffering?'

There is, of course, an argument that an old and ill person might 'appear' to want their life terminated when that is not really their wish; greedy beneficiaries might want to get the inheritance sooner rather than later. Perhaps, in cases such as this, we could require a competent judge to determine the true wishes of that person. It is hard to imagine that such a requirement would overburden our courts as it is unlikely there would be large queues for such a service.

Personally, if my children did not want me around I cannot imagine any reason why I would want to stay anyway.

3 OBTAINING HELP

There are some things that we can do alone and there are many things that we should *only* do alone. However, to expand our potential in respect to self-fulfilment and achieving goals, we need to recruit assistance. A man can build a house alone, but it will be quicker and more efficient if he obtains advice and help.

Help is like a lever. The more help we can obtain, the greater our ability to manipulate and control our environment. Self-interest is the prime motivator in all of us and so it follows that it is in our own interests to use available help. Unfortunately, there is always a cost in obtaining help. Indeed, there is no such thing as a 'free lunch'. The cost may be a simple monetary payment where the debt is liquidated immediately, or it may impose future obligations to return the favour.

'Always go to other peoples' funerals, otherwise they won't come to yours'
Lawrence Peter 'Yogi' Berra (1925–)

As everyone is motivated by self-interest, we must

appeal to the interests of others if we want them to help us. A salesman never sells a vacuum cleaner by pointing out that they need the sale in order to feed their children. They point out how it will help you and how much *you* can't do without it.

Helping others is not a purely altruistic act. There are distinct advantages to us as a result of it. If we all help each other, then we all derive the benefit of the leverage that help provides, and every person has an increased ability to achieve their own personal goals.

It has been said that in order to make a friend, 'let them do you a favour'. The logic of this is that you place yourself under a debt to your potential friend. This leaves them with the feeling that you will return the favour at some later stage and they therefore think more favourably of you. By the same logic, when you help someone else, they immediately feel under an obligation to repay the debt as soon as possible. Thus, helping others is, in fact, very self-serving.

There are numerous methods we can use to obtain help:

1.   We can simply ask (e.g. 'please help me shift a table from one room to the next').

2.   We can persuade others to help.

3.   We can shame another into doing what we want (e.g. 'don't be so selfish!').

4.   We can induce fear into the mind of an unwilling helper (e.g. with a gun to your head I say: 'Give me your wallet!').

The first two methods are well understood and this is how daily commerce is usually transacted. It should also be noted that these methods imply a *quid pro quo* arrangement; in other words, there is a specific payment for the help, or the inference that the helper will receive a similar help at a later time.

The last two methods extract help without ostensibly returning a favour to the helper. If we can get help to achieve our objectives for free, then this is obviously preferable to imposing a commitment on ourselves. If I can get another person to work for me at no cost to myself, then the wealth and fruits of that person's labour accrete to me. If I buy the raw materials, hire the labour and sell the product at a price that pays for all the costs plus a margin of profit, then I have generated this profit for very little personal exertion. The greater the margin between the sale price and the cost of production, the greater the profit and, therefore, the more rapid the accumulation of wealth.

For this reason, we see the methods of shame and induction of fear used extensively by those in authority – parents, politicians and priests.

Courtesy and assistance to others, therefore, has a real purpose in life. It does make life easier for others but, more importantly, it makes life easier and more pleasant for us.

'You cannot hope to build a better world without improving the individuals. To that end each of us must work for his own improvement and at the same time share a general responsibility for all humanity, our particular duty being to aid those to whom we think we can be most useful.'

Marie Curie (1867-1934)

Our Adversarial Society

Society traditionally encourages competition, but the importance of being competitive is purely a thing that we have been brainwashed into believing. Our rulers tend to be people who have an insatiable thirst for power. Competition with its consequent destruction of rivals is a very useful tool for them.

There are certain advantages in the competitive approach, but there are also many disadvantages. It suits our rulers to have us competing with one another on the old British principle of 'divide and rule'. In a society where only certain selected individuals are permitted to accomplish their objectives, the society receives only a limited contribution. Competition does stimulate the desire to achieve, but it also leads to suppression of the aims of others and a subsequent stratification of the society. As a result, the rulers are at the top, and the poor and underprivileged at the bottom.

One might think that helping a rival will give them a competitive advantage. In the short term this may be true. We need to re-think our society. If we helped each other rather than competed, our entire society would be a richer place as everyone would accomplish their goals. Each of us has some unique talents and goals. Poor education and poor encouragement lead to a lesser capacity of the individual to determine and reach their goals, and thereby a loss to society of contributions that could be made.

How much personal depression and alienation results from people being unable to reach even modest ambitions? How much bullying and interpersonal animosity arises from the idea that one must always prevail over others?

From Help to Dictatorship

It is well-known that, at any meeting, a few individuals always dominate proceedings. The other members, apart from the occasional interjection, remain as passive bystanders. As time goes by, the dominant members will assume or acquire executive positions. In such a way, a stratification of power (otherwise known as a hierarchy or pecking order) develops.

Once people get to executive positions, they soon convince themselves they are there by divine right. Any interference with their objectives is simply an irritation that must be surmounted. This commonly leads to all sorts of infringements on the rights of others even to the point of secretly working against the interests of those they pretend to represent. A city councillor now assumes the right to dictate to the citizen what colour he or she may paint their house; a politician now tells the electors they have no right to question oppressive legislation because they do not understand the 'big picture'.

An executive body therefore develops a life of its own and this becomes more important than its *raison d'etre*. The executives claim to be working for others but act to serve their own interests. The former representatives of the people soon become dictators over those whose votes they have usurped to attain power. In *Animal Farm*, George Orwell paints this picture all too clearly: pigs, originally elected to take over the farm on behalf of the other animals, soon begin to suggest the extermination of those animals that do not fit into their scheme of things.

'Princes aim to rule but all the people ask is that they not be oppressed.'
Machiavelli (1469–1527)

Not everybody wants to be a ruler.

4 | THE RULING CLASSES

When Karl Marx wrote *Das Kapital (Capital)* in 1867, he clearly assumed the ruling class (the Capitalist class or *Bourgeoisie*) to be a fixed set of people. At the time, this was a realistic assumption because late 19th-century England did have relatively fixed classes; if a carpenter you were born, a carpenter you would remain. The Bourgeoisie controlled the means of production, distribution and exchange (money). The other, or lower class, had no such assets and had only their labour to sell. Karl Marx called this class the Proletariat.

Marx saw these two groups as well-defined classes having contrary interests: the Bourgeoisie seeking to exploit the Proletariat, and the Proletariat, in turn, resenting that exploitation. He therefore assumed that the Proletariat would ultimately revolt against their slavery, oust the Bourgeoisie, set up government for the benefit of all (Dictatorship of the Proletariat), and the world would become a paradise without wars, starvation, or misery.

Many of Marx's assumptions were correct. We all know of popular revolutions that have begun when oppressed people find the oppression too burdensome. The revolt of Spartacus and the slaves against the Romans, the French and Russian revolutions and even the American War of Independence were just a few of such uprisings. But there were at least two factors that Marx did not consider: the fact that the ruling class is *not* a fixed group, and the fact that everyone (including the Proletariat) acts out of self-interest.

Our Political Rulers

Many members of the ruling class have come up from lower social levels. An industrious worker may acquire assets and wealth and find themselves in a position of power. Marx had not considered this dynamic and tacitly assumed that the classes remained rigidly defined.

The other human factor neglected by Marx is that of self-interest. No matter how altruistic the original intent, members of the ruling class will eventually (if not right at the outset) decide that their personal interests or objectives must take precedence. Charity, after all, does begin at home. Perhaps Joseph Stalin, who originally trained for the priesthood, began with the idea of creating a proletarian utopia, but like St Paul, he apparently saw the light along the way.

When Marx originally talked of class war and the ultimate victory of the proletariat, he had not considered that the proletarians would re-establish tyranny under another name. Indeed, for those of us who have observed socialists over the years, it is abundantly clear that they do not particularly want socialism; they want the present system, but with themselves in charge.

Rather than a definite group of individuals with a rigid agenda, the ruling class of any country might be likened to a typical sporting club. In a sporting club, members come and go, the executives change and over a period of time the entire membership may be replaced.

However, the club maintains a certain ethos or 'spirit' which continually, but subtly, alters over time. Members entering the club absorb the prevalent spirit and tend to be loyal to it. Sometimes the club will take a direction that many members do not agree with, but this does not alter the loyalty and support for the club overall. In fact, members will tend to support ideas they fundamentally disagree with to ensure the stability of the club. However, if the disagreement is too great, the member will resign, but it usually takes a very severe disagreement to induce a member to do this.

In 1957, a British bureaucrat Cyril Northcote Parkinson, published a book called *Parkinson's Law* (or *Pursuit of Progress*). This book originally enunciated 'Parkinson's Law', which has latterly become plagiarised and expanded as 'Murphy's Law' and 'The Peter Principle'. Although the book was a humorous account of British bureaucracy, it did have some acute insights.

Parkinson noted that once a committee exceeded a certain number (about five), it became ineffective. Once this number is exceeded, a few members begin to dominate the discussions and factions begin to form. If the committee reaches, say twelve, about three to five members will dominate the meeting and the others will either align themselves with one of the dominant members, or be left out of the decision-making process altogether. It therefore behoves a passive member to align themselves with one of the more powerful if they wish to have any input.

If one watches parliamentary question time in Australia, the above process can be seen in action. Ultimately, any government is run by a small number of members and the rest do what they are told. Parliamentary members who appear behind the front-benchers on television will rarely be seen to speak (but they will be seen by their constituents).

The government is determined by the party

acquiring the majority of seats in the Lower House. This government is then dominated by a few senior party members. Democracy is thus corrupted for two reasons:

1. The party acquiring the majority of seats virtually never derives support from even 50% of the voters at a general election.

2. The majority of government parliamentarians have no real say in policy and are afraid to oppose any government line for fear of losing pre-selection for the next election. For this reason they will not hesitate to vote against the interests of their electorate if told to do so. They therefore cease to be representatives of their electorates and become mere salespersons of the party line.

The principle of 'cabinet solidarity' in Australian government does have the effect of getting things done but it often results in some inappropriate decisions and actions. No cabinet member would breach a decision to send troops to war even if they disagreed with it. Ultimately, those who initiate wars face very little inconvenience, win or lose, because they can easily claim that they have personally disagreed with the decision but had to support it due to cabinet solidarity: 'The cock-up was made by the others, not by me.'

If you canvass any electorate, you will be lucky to find 10% of voters who can name their local member, and not a lot more who will know who the Prime Minister is. So, why don't we have a system whereby each party nominates five candidates, and a voting system that allots one seat in a five-member executive government for every 20% of the popular vote gained? Get real! That would result in a democratic government where it would be difficult to corrupt individual members; the interests of all Australians would be considered in any decision, laws favouring political allies would be exposed to the public, secret foreign treaties would be almost impossible and Australian soldiers could not be sent to die for the glory of ambitious politicians!

With age, people naturally progress from the social conscience and impecuniosity of the student to the cynical but comfortable middle age of the corporate executive.

'A man who is not a socialist at 20 has no heart; a man who is still a socialist at 40 has no head'

Aristide Briand (1862–1932)

The Australian Federal Parliamentary system consists of two houses: a Lower House (the House of Representatives), and an Upper House (the Senate). Why does it have two houses? What company in Australia votes in a board of directors to run the company and have a second board to stop the first one functioning? The Queensland parliament has only one house and it functions just as well as any other Australian legislature.

The two-house system derives from the British pattern of a House of Commons and a House of Lords. The *raison d'être* of the House of Lords was to retain the power of the aristocrats in the legislative system. However, our Senate has no such function. The Senate was supposed to protect the power of the smaller individual states and act as a 'house of review'. Nowadays, it serves neither of these functions and it has become either a 'house of obstruction' or a rubber stamp.

The Australian people believe they live in a democracy, and it is probably a good thing that they do not know any better. It is, perhaps, not so clear what price we are all paying for the protection of our governmental sinecures and dictatorship. If we replaced the two hundred and forty or so members of parliament with five, if we did away with the charade called 'parliamentary debate' and the horde of hangers-on associated with parliament and its members, how much would we save?

And what about the monarchy? Whether you agree or disagree with the monarchy, the fact is that you cannot have a monarchy and a democracy co-existing. By definition, a monarchy is a rule by one person and a democracy is a rule by the people. If you want a monarchy, fine, but don't pretend that you can also have a democracy simultaneously.

With a monarchy, there is *one* person who can overturn the wishes of a 'democratically elected' government. There are those who would argue that the monarch should never remove a democratically elected government but if one agrees with this argument, the rules need to be changed. If someone has a power that they ought not to have, then that power needs to be legislated out of existence. There is no point in *hoping* that a person in power will act according to any principles of a fair play.

If a power exists, it will ultimately be used.

Denial

Governments and cabinets are microcosms of the ruling classes. Denial of responsibility and support of unprincipled behaviour is a regrettable part of politics. Is it fair to blame a clothing manufacturer for using sweat-shop labour to produce their garments? If they do not do so, their competitors *will* and the manufacturer will be driven out of business. A politician offers the same argument.

In political parties, we commonly hear members declaring that they are 'team players'. Because of the natural self-interest of all individuals, this affirmation is clearly nonsense, but the charade suits everyone. As every member of any political party has their own aspirations to the top position, each of them wants the others to continue to be the 'team players' when they get there.

Another phenomenon that has become exceedingly common with our political rulers is that of *denial*. Where something is too difficult to tackle or where there is a reluctance to pay the real cost of dealing with it, our governments simply deny there is a problem.

Two of the most preferred phrases of denial used by our politicians are: *'There is no Aboriginal problem'* and *'Australia is not a racist country'*.

'There is no Aboriginal problem'

In general, Aboriginals have always been treated as less than equals by the white community in Australia. It is only recently that Aboriginals have been included in the Census, have been able to vote and have been given the right to drink alcohol.

Where governments have taken formal possession of territory, Aboriginals have no right to claim that territory. Where land is allotted to Aboriginals, that land is certainly of no use to non-indigenous Australian commercial interests and is usually pretty useless to the Aboriginals as well. The allocation of land to Aboriginals and the whole question of such land claims have been purely political. It is used by politicians as a vote-winner on the pretence that they care. The High Court has already pointed out that the whole question of Aboriginal land claims could be abolished if the Federal Government simply claimed all non-alienated land once and for all. But for governments, votes are more important than social problems.

Territory has always been owned by whoever could conquer and defend that land. The continent of Australia has been conquered by white man and it is the white man who is able to defend it. Historically, then, Australia belongs to the white man. This may not be how land *should* be owned or distributed but it is the way land *is* owned and distributed.

The system of forcing different ethnic groups to live in separate communities is called *Apartheid* ('separate development'). Australia is thus developing into a nation of two separate classes of citizens Commonwealth intervention into Aboriginal communities whereby social security payments are controlled is an insult. There are certainly problems in Aboriginal communities but these are directly due to the lack of government support for the advancement of these communities. Proper support would not win any votes because it would cost taxpayer money and no-one would notice or care about the results.

We have said sorry and that has fixed it, hasn't it? The reality is that our attitude towards the Aboriginals has not changed in two hundred years. We still treat them as a sub-human race. We are sorry alright – sorry that they are still around to inconvenience us. Our politicians stand in the parliament and, with their eyes almost brimming with tears, proclaim how sorry they are. But what have these politicians done to improve the situation? Nothing! And why not? They have postured for votes and said sorry. Anything else would cost time or money.

Why are we saying sorry for something we had nothing to do with? How can anyone apologise for someone else's sins? Why don't we do something about the crimes being committed by us today so that we won't need another bunch of hypocrites saying 'sorry' in fifty years' time.

'We are not racist'

All governments promote national pride. Of course, we are all proud of our respective countries. That is nothing to be ashamed of any more than being proud of our homes or our parents. The problem arises when we take that national pride to the extreme of believing that we are superior to people of other nations. But this is encouraged by our rulers because it allows them to discriminate and wage wars against others. Our rulers therefore openly deny racism while tacitly encouraging it.

Australia is certainly a racist country. Simply denying this truth allows it to flourish unchecked. Since the Second World War, Australia has had a series of waves of immigrants of different ethnic groups. First, there were the 'Balts', the immigrants from the Baltic states of Latvia, Lithuania and Estonia. Then the Italians, Greeks, Indians, and Vietnamese followed. All of these groups have initially suffered greater or lesser degrees of isolation and discrimination in Australia.

Latterly, we have the 'boat people', often refugees from nations that our government, in its wisdom, has waged war against without any sensible reason. We are told that Australians will decide *who comes into our country and the terms under which they shall come*, but this is not a choice we gave to the countries we bombed and destroyed. Presumably they are not *Ubermensch* like ourselves. We can spend millions of dollars sending our navy to rescue a lone British sailor who is touring the world for sport, but we can't accommodate poor refugees who have risked their lives travelling hundreds of miles over dangerous seas to escape a terror that we inflicted on their country.

Years ago, a politician called Pauline Hanson decried the influx of Asian migrants. She was maligned and persecuted for her stance. But our politicians were quick to embrace the popularity of her views. Our present stance against boat people is unadulterated Pauline Hanson policy.

Attacks on Lebanese, Jews, or Indians are only the acts of a few miscreants, aren't they? Whenever any nation puts itself forward as being better than any other nation, then that nation *is* racist. If I maintain that Australia is the best country in the world, I imply that all other nations are inferior.

Alcoholics Anonymous is an organisation that aids alcoholics, but the first requirement, in order to receive help from this organisation, is that you must admit that you are an alcoholic. There is no point in telling them you are just a bit of a boozer and would like to reduce your intake; if you are not an alcoholic, they will simply tell you to go away and come back when you are.

The point of the example above is that you cannot tackle a problem until you admit that the problem exists. Until we admit that we do have problems with the Aboriginals and racism, we have no hope of resolving these issues. Of course, our politicians continue with their denial because this gains them votes and saves them the effort of having to deal with it.

Our Religious Rulers.

Our religious rulers are another group of rulers within our community. They wield political power in the same way politicians do. They are less obvious as rulers but they do accrete power and divert the fruits of other people's labour unto themselves. The Catholic Church, for example, is one of the richest organisations in the world. Even though many of its adherents are dirt poor and starving, none of its princes go hungry.

The clergy and cult leaders also use the same tried and true methods of instilling fear. Religions and cults have developed as a result of the fears that we all have in respect to the unknown, the incomprehensible, and the future.

We were told that if everyone obeyed the Ten Commandments, our world would be a wonderful place. If we look more closely at these commandments, we find that they are perfectly suited to protect our rulers against us. 'Thou shalt not steal', 'Thou shalt not covet' and 'Thou shalt not kill'—a more perfect set of rules could not be derived to protect a person who has already stolen possessions of others and accreted great wealth. They, of course, will go to hell for what they have done, but you will go to heaven for allowing them to expropriate your property or your spouse without killing them.

Our clerical rulers set the rules and morals that suit their own interests. People are told that if they don't abide by these rules, there will be a judge waiting to punish them. In this way, injustice during one's lifetime will be recompensed by the Lord in the afterlife. The meek shall inherit the earth, but not just now.

There are very powerful political reasons why the clergy should promote a belief in God. It is a very simple way of coercing people into doing as they wish without too much argument and resistance. It is therefore important not to allow anyone to test God or his existence because people may rapidly come to the undesirable conclusion that they are being lied to. Prevent the investigation of cloning because if any damn fool can create life, the mystery of God will suffer a considerable setback.

It is notable that the control of religion has always remained in the hands of the rulers. Priests always occupy a position of domination over the masses. In ancient Egypt, the pharaoh claimed to be a God; in Europe of the middle ages, kings claimed to have a 'divine right'. Henry VIII of England took control of the state religion to suit his own interests. The monarch of England today is the governor of the Church of England.

Perhaps we should question the sincerity of our rulers as they seem to have no hesitation in assassinating their opponents or waging wars and spilling innocent blood when it suits their interests. The whole panoply of claims and exhortations of the Judeo-Christian-Islamic religions are no different from the claims made by the leaders of any modern-day religious sect. All of the latter-day sect leaders claim to provide great things in the afterlife and they all declare themselves to be the only path to that life after death. None of them can or do provide any evidence for their claims. They all require donations of money (lots of it) and usually access to numerous women for sexual favours. As we were taught that monogamy is a virtue, there seems to be no logic in God singling out cult leaders to indulge in intercourse with multiple partners.

The main feature of most religions is some belief in an afterlife. This is because we all have an over-inflated idea of our own importance: 'Surely, no cat or pigeon could be as important as me'; 'A life as important as mine could surely not end as insignificantly as that of a leaf falling from a tree'.

Although we may wish to believe in our own importance and immortality, there is no rational evidence to support these beliefs. However, the wish to believe and the fear of what might happen if we don't, has opened the door to the clergy and other cult leaders. They assure us that all of our beliefs are true and that our hopes will be realised - if we follow their leadership.

To add a sweetener to the idea of an afterlife, warrior religions such as those of Islam and the Norse had rewards for warriors who died in battle. In the Norse religions, warrior maidens, the Valkyries, would carry the warrior killed in battle to Valhalla where they would administer to his sensual needs in a manner befitting such a hero. Islamic warriors are promised a supply of virgins awaiting them as a reward for their efforts. But, virgins have a very short shelf-life. What happens to these virgins after defloration? Are they sent to a nunnery and replenished each morning? I am not opposed to the concept in principle, but what is the purpose of such a union in an afterlife and who looks after the kids?

However, as no one has ever come back from the afterlife to disprove any claims about it, it is a pretty hard argument to counter.

PART II

PSYCHOLOGICAL PRESSURES
USED BY OUR RULERS

5 | TRUTH

As we are concerned with lies that we are being told, we need to clarify what we mean by *truth*. We can consider truth as a type of map. A traveller will use a map to plan an optimal path across terrain. If the map is accurate, a traveller can plan the most efficient path from A to B. In this way, they can enjoy the best features of the trip and avoid the dangers such as precipices and raging rivers. On the other hand, a traveller does not need an accurate map of an area they are not traversing — if I choose to hike in Tasmania, it is of no concern to me that a map of Queensland might be totally inaccurate.

In life, truth serves the same purpose. If we have the full facts about a given situation, we can then determine the best course of action or the best type of response to that situation. The two most controversial topics of discussion are *politics* and *religion*. The reason they are controversial is that no-one has all of the facts and the debate consists mainly of personal surmises.

There are at least two circumstances in which the truth is of no concern to us:

1. If we have no need to respond.

2. If the information is of no benefit to us.

An example of the first circumstance occurs when a politician is found to be having an affair with their secretary. What response is necessary? Who cares? Of course, their political opponents will spread the word widely in the hope of discrediting and possibly displacing them. When faced with some accusation of impropriety that is of a private nature, the best response of a politician should be: 'It's none of your business'.

Information is of no benefit when it may be hurtful to the recipient. Let us say that a very dear friend of yours is on his deathbed. As he is sinking, he takes your hand, thanks you for your loyalty and mentions that you are the only associate that has never tried to hit on his wife. What would then be the use of you telling him the truth that, in fact, you have been having an affair with his wife for years and that there is some question about the parentage of his children?

From earliest childhood, we are taught to tell the truth at all times. What is more, we have all been conditioned to expect pain if we do not tell the truth. We therefore undergo psychological stress whenever we tell a lie. It is the physiological changes which occur as a result of this that makes a lie detector useful.

There is one societal group which has a very definite interest in always being able to extract the truth: the ruling class. For example, picture a government that wants to put a freeway through a certain sensitive area. If some opposition arises to this proposition, the government may very well call for community input. The average person in the street might regard this as democracy in action. In reality, it is usually a device to subvert democracy. The government has already decided its course of action and wants to know what opposition arguments it has to counter. If a submission shows that a freeway should not be built because it would endanger the lesser-horned collywobble, they will be able to counter that any other course would wipe out the even rarer and more valuable triple-breasted bodenheimer. The residents will always be told that their submission has been considered but there are a number of reasons why their reasons are not valid (not the least of which is that a common mortal like you cannot be expected to understand the 'big picture'). There are always a number of good reasons why a toxic waste dump should be installed in your city — the overriding one being that you live in an electorate that is not necessary for the re-election of the government. It is therefore wise to understand the reasons behind the call for public submissions and not waste your time providing any.

Courts of law require the truth to be told. This is a reasonable requirement for an impartial jury as this panel needs to know the entire truth in order to come to a fair and just decision. However, most people do not want a *fair* decision — they want a *favourable* decision. In such cases, selective lapses of memory seem inordinately common. It is amazing how many politicians can remember the entire speech by an opponent on April 5 1983, but can't remember who gave them the brown paper bag full of money last Tuesday.

There are practical reasons for telling the truth. If someone needs true information in order to make a proper judgement or take a specific course of action, they should be given that truth. If an individual needs to know they are dying of cancer in order to set their affairs in order – the truth should not be concealed from them. But if a person asking for the truth has no need of it except to damage someone else's prospects, there is no requirement to give it to them, and there is probably an ethical requirement not to do so.

Propaganda

Propaganda is the material used to propagate a doctrine. Its purpose is to convince people to a particular point of view, so by definition, it only transmits one side of an argument. The essence of good propaganda is that it must always contain a *kernel of truth*.

If a government wants to induce its citizens to invade Iraq, it might make the following statements:

1. Iraq has weapons of mass destruction.
2. Iraq can deploy these weapons within 45 minutes.
3. The Iraqi people will greet our troops as liberators.

The real reasons for invading Iraq that we are *not* told by our government are:

1. We *want* control of Iraqi oil.
2. We are associated with the companies that will make a lot of money providing services to Iraq after the war.

The initial statements are used to induce fear into the recipient minds so that logical analysis is counteracted. A typical response by majority people would be: 'Such weapons must be removed and we are happy for our government to do what is necessary to protect us. What is more, we are doing the Iraqi people a favour, they want us to invade and liberate them.'

If people, on the other hand, analyse these statement logically, they would come to the following conclusions:

1. What types of weapons are being called the 'weapons of mass destruction'? A machine gun also fits into the strict definition, but we are being led by propaganda

to assume that the weapons are probably much more horrendous.

2. All weapons of mass destruction that Iraq may have (chemical, biological, etc.) were provided to Iraq by the US government. (One US commentator has said, 'We know exactly what weapons of mass destruction Iraq has — we have the receipts'.)

3. If Iraq could deploy its lethal weapons in 45 minutes, one would have to take control in 40 minutes to avoid disaster. It never occurred to anyone that three months of preparation to invade was somewhat illogical.

4. It is rare for any nation to want foreigners to invade them no matter how tyrannical their government is.

So soldiers blithely went to fight and die in Iraq believing they were doing a service to the country and humanity. Had they been told the other side of the argument, they might have been less enthusiastic.

The above situation exemplifies why, in court, a witness is asked to tell 'the truth, the whole truth and nothing but the truth'. Where the whole truth is not told, one is quoting the situation 'out of context' and this may be misleading. If one tells other than the truth, this will clearly mislead.

This brings us to abuses of the dissemination of truth by various media outlets, especially the press. Journalists are fond of claiming that certain salacious, and usually libellous, information is published because it is 'in the public interest'. There is a significant difference between something that the public might be interested in and something that is 'in the public interest'.

The expression 'in the public interest' suggests that the information is something the public needs to know in order to make informed decisions. This is often very different to something that the public might be interested in. For instance, the public (including myself) is always interested in knowing anything salacious about anybody, but that does not mean that the public *needs* to know it. The press often uses this confusion about public interest to justify publishing any scurrilous information that will magnify the sales of its printed material. Freedom of the press is vital for freedom of every individual, but by abusing its position purely in the pursuit of revenue, the press invites the greater danger of censorship and the animosity of its readership.

Whenever anyone is trying to swing you to their point of view, it is important to analyse the other side of the argument no matter how painful or burdensome that may be. Most words have two meanings: a *technical* and an *emotional* one. For example, 'insurgent' and 'freedom fighter' technically both mean the same thing. Emotionally, however, an insurgent is a 'baddie' and a freedom fighter is a 'goodie'. You can do the same analysis on 'I am strong-willed' versus 'You are stubborn' and many other such phrases. If you wish to avoid being hoodwinked by propaganda, always replace strongly-emotional words with neutral ones and re-evaluate your response. For example, you could replace both 'insurgent' and 'freedom fighter' with 'soldier'. In this way, it will usually become clear how the propagandist is setting out to sway your judgement.

When Iraq invaded Kuwait and the US intervened, we were naturally fed the propaganda line that everything the Americans did was moral and everything the Iraqis did was evil. We even had the spectacle of a Kuwaiti princess tearfully describing on television how Iraqi soldiers had entered a nursery, tipped the babies out of humidicribs and taken the humidicribs away. Because the western world *wanted* to believe that Iraqi soldiers would do such a thing, no one really batted an eyelid at the revelation. The whole event was later proven to be an utter fabrication but it suited the propaganda purpose at the time.

One major problem in world politics is the propaganda that our side can do no wrong and that anyone who opposes us is evil. We find journalists today who seem to be amazed that the people of Nazi Germany allowed their government to persecute Jews, while the same journalists accept, without question, the propaganda of their own governments which presently and unjustly persecutes Muslims. Why wouldn't the people of Nazi Germany trust and accept the propaganda of their government? We do exactly the same thing today.

The word 'terrorist' is a highly emotional word describing someone who instils extreme fear. Are we to believe that people who blow up railway stations are terrorists but those who drop bombs from 10,000 feet are not? Or is terror something that can only be experienced by those on our side of a conflict?

The excuse for instituting the second Gulf War against Saddam Hussein was classic one-sided propaganda. The World Trade Center in New York was bombed by two civilian planes with the loss of some 3,000 lives. That act was wrong and it is to be deprecated. But to relate the World Trade Center bombing with the later US bombing of Afghanistan or the invasion of Iraq defies any reasonable logic. If an Australian criminal or a criminal organisation happened to bomb the White House in Washington, would we expect the US to take revenge action by bombing Sydney? Of course not! So why do we accept the US bombing of Afghanistan as a reprisal? The attack on the World Trade Center was equivalent to the dropping of two or three bombs on the US — the attacks on Afghanistan and Iraq amounted to thousands of bombs being dropped there in return. Because of the propaganda, most people expressed a horror at the attack on the US. However, we have no feelings at all about the human suffering due to our attacks on Iraq because we are never shown any pictures of the suffering that we inflict on our enemies. Our own suffering is, however, always graphically and extensively portrayed.

Again, we must look to what we have been conditioned to believe: Afghans, Muslims and Taliban are different to us. The loss of their lives is unimportant to us (and besides they have been at war for so long that a few more deaths won't make any difference to them either). As a consequence, the bombing is acceptable. But even if this argument had any logic to it, we would have to draw an impossibly long bow to justify the bombing of Afghanistan or Iraq as retaliation for the World Trade Center attack!

The proposition that politicians should be entitled to start wars without question should strike fear into the hearts of every thinking person.

In the days of the 'cold war' between the Soviet Union and the US, a Korean airline passenger jet was shot down by a Soviet fighter aircraft after venturing over Sakhalin Island. Again, the propaganda line was used to show the Soviets to be evil, 'how could any decent person shoot down a passenger jet that had simply made a mistake and gone off course?' The Australian Prime Minister was loud in his condemnation within hours of receiving the news. As more of the truth trickled out, the event became more and more suspicious.

Sakhalin Island is a well-known Soviet military installation, and the pilot, a Korean national, must have known that. The plane was hundreds of kilometres off course and this could not have been accidental. The time the plane spent over Sakhalin could not have occurred just as a result of a simple over-flight. The Soviet authorities could hardly be blamed for preventing their military installations becoming tourist destinations. One is forced to come to the unfortunate conclusion that a civilian airliner was used as a spy plane and the lives of its passengers were gambled in order to obtain intelligence information. After this, can any citizen trust their governments not to sacrifice them when and if it suits them?

Let us contrast the brouhaha of the Korean airlines flight with the incident of a US warship downing an Iranian domestic jet in the Persian Gulf. In the latter case, it was an 'accident' and no more was heard of it. One can hardly imagine that propaganda surrounding the Korean airlines incident would have stopped if the Soviet authorities had really shot it down accidentally.

In order to protect ourselves against being duped by propaganda, we must be alert to the circumstances in which we will succumb to propaganda without much resistance:

1. Whenever any proposition threatens our beliefs, we fiercely defend those beliefs because this is an attack on our ego. We are unlikely to listen to or analyse anything which is contrary to our beliefs, no matter how compelling the logic. Our belief system comprises ideas that we have been taught to believe and ideas we have come to believe on the basis of our experience.

'A man convinced against his will, remains of the same opinion still.'

Anon

2. Where propaganda fits into our belief system, we are at greatest risk because this is when we are least likely to question it. If I have been taught to believe that Iraqis are monsters, I will be unlikely to question the suggestion that they may have killed Kuwaiti babies. But if you made the same suggestion regarding Australian soldiers, I would be looking for more evidence than your simple word of mouth. Our egos and belief systems can therefore work against the

search for truth and, in the world of politics, this can be extremely dangerous to world peace.

Whenever presented with only one side of an argument, always look for the opposing arguments. In other words, be a 'devil's advocate'; treat the propaganda as being false in the first instance and derive the arguments that would support this premise. Often, a piece of propaganda that is analysed this way will ultimately be found to hold no water.

6 F E A R

Fear is the universal currency of control

Once we can instil in the minds of our followers a fear of some future event or danger with the belief that we can protect them from it, we are in business. One of the most important natural drives in all animals is that of self-preservation — protect yourself first and deal with any consequences later.

When faced with any unusual situation, it is wise to be cautious. Therefore, it is not difficult for politicians to convince us that any selected foreigner is dangerous. In spite of all the political hype, your chances of being harmed by a terrorist are less than your chances of being struck by lightning. Yet billions of dollars of *your* money is being spent to protect *you* from terrorists. How much money is being spent protecting you from lightning? Note that it is *your* money that is being spent to manufacture fear in your mind against an imaginary danger.

Fear is an emotional response. Once emotion comes in the door, logic goes out the window. Once fear is induced, it won't matter that the suggested protection might be nonsense. Any protection is better than none. If I am afraid that a terrorist might harm me, I won't care if everyone around me is gaoled or if everyone in a turban is summarily executed — as long as there is a chance that these measures might protect me. How simple now to deprive anyone of natural justice. The Australian government has recently introduced draconian laws that deprive accused 'terrorists' of the basic legal rights given to any proven murderer. These laws give the authorities the right to arrest (and even murder) any person under a suspicion of terrorism without being answerable to any court or having to disclose the information about detaining the person concerned. Yet, nobody seems to challenge the concept that this is 'reasonable for our protection'. In reality, these laws can be used against any opponent of the ruling regime.

When our rulers instil fear, it is usually about some future event. We all have some nervousness about the future as it has not already happened, and there is no likelihood that you can prove them wrong because nobody knows what the future will bring.

'Never trust anyone who pretends to be able to predict the future.'
Anon

Politicians commonly use fear as a weapon against their opponents: 'If you vote for my opponent, they will destroy your life-style, raise interest rates, etc.' There is never any real evidence that these things will occur nor is there any evidence that you will avoid the same fate if you vote for the politician making the claim. Presently, we are exposed to the fear of Muslim 'fanatics' and 'fundamentalists': Islam is a dangerous religion and Muslims wear strange clothes — they must surely be evil. This fear of Muslims is reinforced daily by our politicians and news media. As a result we accept the right of our armed forces to wreak carnage on hapless Afghanis and

Iraqis without question.

Every religion is based on fear. Without fear, no western religion would survive. The churches have always used fear to keep the flock in line. During the first half of the 20th century, Catholic children were terrorised with the fear of hellfire and damnation if they dared to sin. As time has gone by, less people have accepted this extreme fear-mongering. It is also of interest that since the fear element has diminished, so have attendances at churches.

But now that you are no longer frightened of eternal punishment, the religious leaders advance the fear that disobedience will separate you from God for all eternity. Why people should fear not being in the presence of a being they have never met and who has never given any evidence of His existence is an interesting question.

As fear is an emotional issue, logic is counteracted. This gives us a marvellous ability to quarantine ideas. We can decry a lack of logic in one area but blissfully accept the same lack of logic in another. We can accept 'visions' seen by biblical characters as divine revelations but regard visions seen by present-day acquaintances as lunacy.

In respect to religion, fear relates to the future, specifically to the period after death. Logic surely demands that we should be equally concerned about where we were before we were born. The reason why we have no concern for prior existences is that whatever happened then is in the past. An after-life, on the other hand, is in the future and may become unpleasant.

Western religions use a 'stick and carrot' method of control. The stick is the fear of eternal damnation and the carrot is a promise of 'heaven'. The Catholic Church has made allowances for their devout ladies by promising that they will become 'brides of Christ'. How Christ was induced to agree to this polygamous duty, I don't know, but I am sure the Church would never promise anything that could not be delivered. Anyway, we don't need women to fight wars so why waste time promising them anything.

Religious leaders infer that they have a special relationship with God and that they are our 'passport to heaven'. They therefore take it upon themselves to enforce God's purported rules. The intimidation and tortures of the Spanish Inquisition are only one example. To my knowledge, there is no admonition in the scriptures that gives church leaders this authority. There is a big difference between 'go unto the four corners of the earth and preach my gospel' and 'torture and belt the bejesus out of them if they don't listen'.

We need to understand that the fear created by our rulers is a fraud and a deceit. Our potential is forever crippled by fear of what we are told might be. When exposed to fear tactics, the first question to ask is: 'Why is this person or organisation trying to frighten me?' The answer will usually expose the emptiness and absurdity of the threat. It will also open your eyes to what the fear-mongers hope to gain for themselves.

'Nothing in life is to be feared, it is only to be understood. Now is the time to understand more, so that we may fear less.'
Marie Curie (1867–1934)

7 | GOOD AND EVIL

Let's start this chapter on Good and Evil with an example. You and I go to an art gallery to look at a painting of a woman that has been recommended to us. I believe that the image of a woman is quite beautiful but you think otherwise. How can this be? How can the painting be both beautiful and ugly at the same time? The answer leads us into the depths of philosophy that has been argued for over 2,500 years.

It brings us to the concepts of *subjectivity* and *objectivity*. An object is the same object no matter who looks at it. A picture is a picture. But if I now describe it as a 'beautiful' picture, I am investing it with a quality it does not inherently possess — I am making a *subjective* evaluation.

Words can have two meanings: a *technical* and an *emotional* meaning. Let us examine two statements:

1.   'I am a devout Christian.'
2.   'He is a Muslim fundamentalist.'

Both refer to individuals who take their religion

seriously and, on the surface, the statements have no technical difference in meaning except that one is a Christian and one is a Muslim. But the emotional impact of each statement is entirely different, isn't it? In the first statement, I am putting myself forward as a normal upright citizen whom you can trust. In the second statement, I am inviting you to be careful of a person who is dangerous and who might cut off your hands if you inadvertently pick up his lunch box.

This exemplifies the danger of not being aware when subjective statements are made. Whenever faced with a statement that creates an *emotional* response, be very alert to the possibility that it is *subjective*. The purpose of subjective statements is to precondition people to come to a desired conclusion without offering any proof. Once you have heard and accepted without question that a person is a 'Muslim fundamentalist', it is now dead easy to convince you that he or she should be arrested, held without trial and that they should have no right to the normal processes of justice.

This injustice is bad enough but it has even more serious repercussions: once you are convinced of the dangers of the 'Muslim fundamentalist', there is no problem to induce you to join the army and go off to foreign lands to kill such dangerous people. And you are prepared to do all of this without one skerrick of evidence.

In *The Republic*, Plato discusses good and evil at some length. He starts with the proposition that I would define a good man as one who looks after my interests and harms my enemies. But what about my enemy? A good man to my enemy is one who would harm me. In fact, whether a man is bad or good is entirely subjective and dependent upon the point of view of the person making the judgement.

'Beauty is in the eye of the beholder'
Lord Byron (1788–1824)

There is no such thing as 'good' or 'evil'. The concepts of good and evil are *abstract* and *subjective* and have no objective reality.

When President Reagan once said that the Soviet Union was an 'evil empire', he was really saying: 'This regime doesn't suit me'. When President Bush stated that certain countries are part of an 'axis of evil', he was simply saying that they did not conform to his interests. To me, therefore, something is good if I like it and it is in my interests. However, that which is good to me may be evil to you.

When our rulers tell us that something is 'evil', they invite us to accept that it is also bad for us. However, that which does not suit their interests might very well suit us down to the ground. We must not be fooled into believing that something is inherently evil simply because our rulers say it is. It is therefore worth repeating that if you are subjected to a word that elicits a strong emotional response, replace it with one of neutral emotional impact and analyse the statement again.

Throughout history, humankind has devised abstract concepts and attempted to put them forward as real entities. Wealth and beauty are surely abstract, society-made concepts. So is the idea that gold has more intrinsic value than a base metal and yet it is only a matter of a century or two ago that alchemists were trying to transmute base metals into gold. The concepts of *good* and *evil* are also society-made, abstract and subjective.

This brings us to the concept of *morality*. The word derives from the Latin word *mores* – a *custom*. Morality has many definitions but the common ones are:

1.   Morality is a code of 'right' or 'good' conduct.

2.   Morality concerns itself with the distinction between good and evil.

As good and evil are purely subjective, let us regard moral conduct as conduct which promotes harmony with others but does not interfere with their rights. This being so, we can recognise two distinct classes: *private morality* and *public morality*.

1.   *Private morality* is of a personal nature where an individual chooses to act in a way that involves only themselves or others who willingly consent. If I decide to commit suicide, this affects only me and it is none of your business. Even though the state has never been given a mandate to interfere in areas of private morality, it nevertheless does so.

2.   *Public morality* involves actions where other people are or might be affected without their consent. In this category we can include murder or driving on a particular side of the road. The state and the law have a legitimate interest in directing or controlling such activities on behalf of those who might be adversely affected.

Because these two types of morality are confused, the daily lives of many people are interfered with by those who would seek to impose their personal moral views on others. If those being harassed at abortion clinics decided to blockade churches and interfered with the freedoms of right-to-life worshippers, you can imagine the screams of indignation.

For harmony in a community, one has to accept the right of each individual to his or her own views and the right of each person to act as he or she chooses providing they are not acting to the detriment of anyone else. We may not agree with those views and we may not choose to act in the same way ourselves, but if we are not prepared to accord sovereignty to others, we cannot validly argue against them imposing their views on us if they obtain the power to do so.

8|GOD

'Man is the only animal who has created a god after his own image.'

Anon

If we accept that 'good' and 'evil' are objective and concrete, it is then not hard to imagine that there might be an embodiment of these concepts in the forms of a *God* and a *Devil*. Because 'good' and 'evil' are subjective concepts, they have no objective reality. When something is good for one person it may be evil for another. How, then, can God be perfectly good? If God sides with one person, He will often have to act to the detriment of another. The latter person will therefore regard God as evil. For God to be perfectly good, He must be good to all people at all times. This surely presents our theoretical God with a dilemma. His only alternative, surely, is to do no favours for anyone. If there is a God and He is perfectly good, He may not interfere in human affairs. As this is the common experience, perhaps there is a God acting as He logically must.

As God is unable to interfere in human affairs in

order to avoid the charge of favouritism, we have numerous zealots filling in for Him. This leads to the practice of exorcisms and multiple other forms of religious hocus-pocus. We still have wars and genocide waged on behalf of this all-loving God.

In ancient times, one can imagine that people would have found nature rather confusing and unfathomable (and we have certainly not advanced much since then). It would not be surprising for them to accept the concept that some greater intelligence was responsible for all of the creation they saw about them. Anything that they could not understand was placed into the province of the gods. Good things such as harvests and good weather on one hand, and bad things such as storms and floods on the other, could then be blamed on particular gods. There would therefore be good and bad gods depending on what was unleashed on humankind at any given time. It would then follow that acts to propitiate the gods, such as sacrifices, would be worthwhile if this induced the gods to smile on them.

A multitude of gods became quite unwieldy and required laborious observance. At this stage, Zoroaster and our Hebrew brothers came to our aid and created a system that required only one god. This was much more economical and the concept became even more desirable when people realised that the 'true' God would not tolerate competition.

The problem is that no one has ever met the 'true' God. How can we be sure that the God we presently worship is not an imposter? What are the features that we need to look for to ensure that we are dealing with the real McCoy? The only people who can truly be said to be obeying the Commandment 'Thou shalt have no other God before me' are the atheists. If you have *no* God, you certainly can't have one before the true one.

There may or may not be a God. I cannot prove

that there is no God, but then again, nobody can prove that there is one. In fact, in order to prove there is no God, I must, paradoxically, prove that there is one.

Area of knowledge that Humans do not have

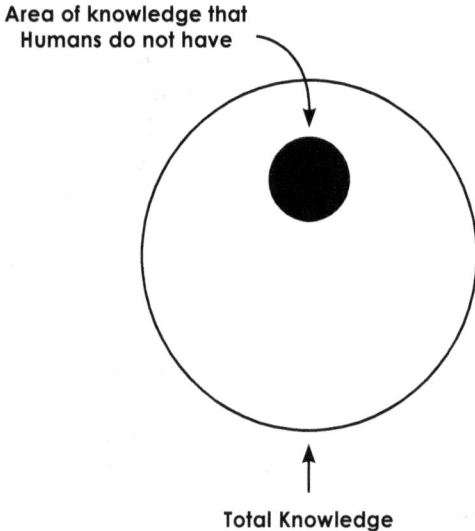

Total Knowledge

Let us say that the sum of total knowledge can be represented by a large circle. Further, let us say that human knowledge consisted of all the knowledge in that circle except for the knowledge represented by the small black circle (which also fits into our concept that we already know pretty much all that there is to know).

Even if there was no evidence of God's existence in the large white circle, God could still exist in the small black circle. Now, if any person possessed total knowledge, including that in the small black circle, *one would be God* by definition. Hence, in order to prove that God does not exist, I must prove that there is a God. Therefore, although I might maintain that there is no proof of the existence of God, I can never prove that God does not exist.

'You can often be proven wrong but you can never prove you are right.'

Richard Feynman (1918–1988), Physicist

The above analogy can be used to show that Feynman's axiom must always be true. We can only prove the truth of something within the sphere of our knowledge. Thus, something we believe today can later be proven wrong as our sphere of knowledge increases. Because we can never know everything, a *proof* that we are right must remain elusive.

Feynman's axiom has a practical use. Let us say that someone devises a theory to explain some natural phenomenon. Presumably, they have some evidence to support their theory. Should they continue to search for more evidence to make this theory watertight? Now, by Feynman's axiom, this will be a waste of time because it does not matter how much evidence they can gather, they can never prove they are right. But it only takes one definite bit of evidence to contradict the theory and their theory is finished.

The lesson, then, is not to waste time looking for supporting evidence, start looking for evidence that contradicts the theory.

We are all free to believe in anything we want. If I choose to believe in the tooth fairy, that is my own business and it cannot possibly harm others unless I impose my belief on them. So, does it matter whether God exists or not? If one lives according to the 'live and let live' principle, none of God's alleged commandments or exhortations would be broken. If we live in this way, there is surely no need to fear any retribution from God whether we believe in Him or not.

Do *I* believe in God? No, not in the accepted sense. I do believe in some extra-human intelligence. When I write, I look at some of the words on the computer and often wonder where they came from. I believe in something beyond us that guides human activity, something like an air traffic controller who guides aeroplanes in a way that provides the most efficient and considerate flow of traffic in the safest manner. If I am going to the bank, I take the view that the powers-that-be will do their best to accommodate me and provide me with a convenient parking space. Most times, a convenient space is available. Sometimes I have to park some distance away; I accept that the powers-that-be had reasons to provide a space for someone else with more urgent need. This eliminates any worry about finding a parking space. Are there really some supernatural powers-that-be? I don't know and it doesn't matter. It works for me.

We are told that God has given us 'free will'. This is the method by which the believers excuse God's non-interference in human affairs. The question therefore needs to be asked — if God has given me free will, by what right does another person take from me a gift given to me by God? By what right does a 'right-to-life' person prevent a woman from exercising her free will to have an abortion if she so desires? Is this God so weak that He is unable to police His own rules?

One day, a man and his wife were playing a round of golf. At one stage, the man unfortunately sliced his golf ball into the rough. When he went to retrieve it, he came across a huge Nubian man wearing a turban. At the Nubian's feet was the missing golf ball beside a shattered bottle.

"Sir, my deepest thanks," said the Nubian. "I am a genie who has been imprisoned within that bottle for many centuries. Your golf ball shattered the bottle and set me free. As a token of my deep appreciation for freeing me, I would like to accord you three wishes. Pray tell, what would your wishes be?"

"Well, I have a wonderful car but it is getting old. Could you

grant me a new one?"

"Most certainly," said the genie. "When you return to the car park after your game, you will find a brand new Rolls Royce in the place where you left your old car. Now, your second wish would be…?"

"My wife and I have always lived in a modest house and I have always wanted to provide her with a better one. Would it be possible to have a new house?"

"No problem at all," said the genie. "When you arrive home, you will find a brand new two-storey home where your old house used to be. Do you have a third and final wish?"

"Kind sir, my wife and I have always lived modestly without many luxuries. If I had one million dollars, I should be the happiest man in the world. Would it be too much to ask for such a favour?"

"Not at all," said the genie. "When you get your next bank statement, you will find an extraordinary deposit of one million dollars before your eyes."

As the man picked up his golf ball, the genie spoke again. "My dear sir," he began, "I notice that you are accompanied by a very attractive lady. As I have been confined to that bottle for so long, you can imagine my pent-up desires. Would it be too much to ask for a small period of time in which I may enjoy your lady's favours?"

The man was taken somewhat aback but felt that he did owe the genie some consideration. He therefore put the proposition to his wife who felt that it was a small price to pay for the generosity shown.

After the genie and the lady had consummated their desires and obligations, the genie asked: "How old is your husband"

"Forty–five."

"Forty-five – and he still believes in genies?"

Whether one believes in God or not, there are many religious stories (as there are many religious works of art) that must surely bring light to the darkest soul. The following is the work of an unknown author:

A man, having passed from this life, found himself in heaven. On speaking to God, he asked why the Lord had never taken an interest in his life.

The Lord pointed to the sands on a beach and said: 'There, my son, is the course of your life. I was always there with you. See that there are two sets of footprints as you travelled along.'

'But, Lord, at the times of most trouble in my life, you deserted me for there I see only one set of footprints.'

'Those were the times that I carried you, my son.'

PART III

CORRUPTION OF OUR INSTITUTIONS

9 | GUIDED DEMOCRACY

We all tend to believe that we live in a democracy and have a vote and some say in the running of our country. This is a delusion. Our votes are not fairly apportioned according to our wishes, nor do we have any say in the management of our country once our votes have been usurped.

Politicians need to acquire power in order to exert their influence. To acquire power, they need to be elected to a seat in parliament. This is achieved by using money to advertise. The chance of success in an election is directly proportional to the money available to spend. Such money comes from those who have it to spare. It follows that politicians will pass laws and guide the economy in the interests of those who provide them with their positions of power. These latter people are not necessarily the average voters but usually industrialists, financiers, and interest groups who can generate money.

The rulers work to support their own interests. This often means working against the interests of the rest of the population. In fact, the wealth generated by the general populace is harnessed to the needs of the rulers.

The average working members of a society have a large proportion of their earnings confiscated as tax. The big industrial corporations remit a very small proportion of their earnings to the tax department. The laws of the country (surprise, surprise) just work out that way.

An average citizen is taught to obey the rules. His or her wealth, however, is plundered by the rulers and their life is forfeit to the state when it becomes necessary to defend or promote the interests of the rulers. We were all taught to regard the truth as inviolable. As a result, one would think that a politician who lied would theoretically be committing political suicide. History shows that quite the reverse is true.

How politicians deceive the voters:

1. *Tell the people what they want to hear.*

The aim of a politician is to get elected. This requires people to vote for him or her, so electors will be told what they want to hear. However, politicians hold their seats by grace of their political party, not because of the voters. If party policy is contrary to public interest, a politician will always do the bidding of their party and will always sell out their electorate in favour of their real master. It is a case of 'he (or she) who pays the piper calls the tune'. After selling out their constituents and losing the next election, they will always assure you that they have heard your views and their policy is now in line with that. (This poor sense of hearing prior to an election and the miraculous subsequent recovery has never been satisfactorily explained.) People want to believe what they are told. If you tell the people what they want to hear, you can expect success.

There is no general law against lying. When a politician is caught out lying, they confesses that they made a simple 'mistake', sheds a crocodile tear or two and then offers the sincerest heart-felt apology. Sometimes they will claim they didn't really lie – you simply misheard them. If a politician knows that you will definitely not vote for them if they tell the truth (but you might vote for them if they lie), then they have nothing to lose by lying. The careers of many politicians have advanced every time that they lied. One politician I knew promised a police station in one locality of his electorate for three successive elections. There still is no police station there.

2.   *Nobody cares about truth or lies unless they have a direct effect on the listener.*

We have all been exposed to multiple documentaries on the bombing of the World Trade Center in New York. We have seen the tears in the eyes of the witnesses; the anguish of relatives. We are all affected; we are angered! But what of the American bombing of Afghanistan and Iraq? Tens of thousands of innocent people have lost, and continue to lose their lives and suffer there. But because we do not see the tears and the grief of their loss, this has no effect on us. We don't care because we don't know.

3.   *The mandate.*

A wonderful little catch-all is the 'mandate' (the word derives from the Latin *mandatum* – an order). The policy platform of any party contains many different offers. At an election, people presumably consider the parts of a given political-party A's policy that suits them. If these suitable parts outweigh the unsuitable parts and also outweigh the suitable parts of any other party—B, C or D—then party A will get their vote. Nobody embraces the entire policy of any party nor does any political party command much more than 50% of the popular vote. It is therefore laughable for any politician or a political party to claim that they have a specific 'mandate' for any particular legislation.

In the early 1970s, the Federal Labor Government claimed a mandate to introduce a universal health insurance system known at the time as Medibank. They could not get this bill through the Senate and ultimately, a double dissolution of both houses of Parliament occurred. Even after that dissolution, the Labor government did not gain the control of the Senate, but because of the rules of double dissolution, it was able to force the bill through. If the normal rights of Senators had not been waived by the dissolution, the bill would not have passed. The introduction of Medibank ushered in the progressive destruction of the Australian health delivery system.

If a politician offered to provide free meat, would you vote for them? Of course you would. Perhaps he or she won't keep their promise but the chances of them providing free meat is certainly greater than the opponent who is not even making the offer. People will therefore be swayed by political promises and, because they are used to politicians using weasel words they will not be terribly disappointed if the promises don't come to fruition.

'Politicians' promises are like pie-crusts—only made to be broken.'
V. I. Lenin (1870–1924)

How votes are manipulated and usurped:

In Australia, voting can also be manipulated by those who know how. The following examples show some methods by which our politicians corrupt democracy and cheat the citizen of this vote:

1.   *The electoral roll.*

In any electorate, there is a list of eligible voters known

as the 'electoral roll'. After a while, this list becomes somewhat incorrect as it comes to contain the names of people who have left the district or died, while the names of new eligible voters may not have been added to the roll.

Electoral officials make some attempt to ensure the accuracy of the rolls but this diligence is not all that zealous, particularly at the level of local councils. Huge discrepancies can often be found. That dead people can still remain on the rolls is curious when one considers that those on the roll who do not vote are usually subject to a fine. Why aren't these names deleted at this time? And why do they stay on the roll for subsequent elections? The advice is clear: 'Vote early and vote often' (but get a list of the different names that you need to assume).

2. *The preferential voting system.*

This system requires the voter to number every candidate in order of the voter's preference. The reason touted is that, if your first choice does not get up, you can list a second, third or a further preference. Sounds good. But the reality is somewhat different. If you have to vote for every candidate, it is possible that your vote can ultimately be used to elect a candidate that you certainly did not want. This suits the major parties; they all know that one of them will eventually get your vote.

3. *The 'running mate'.*

Because of the preferential system, it behoves a reasonably strong candidate to get a weaker candidate to stand with the understanding that the weaker candidate will recommend to voters to give their second preferences to the stronger candidate. Voters who know the weaker candidate, and probably would otherwise not vote for the stronger candidate, will thereby be induced to give their preferences to the stronger candidate and hence increase his or her chances of victory. This same effect occurs when stronger political parties make deals with weaker parties for preferences, or weaker parties make deals with stronger parties for later political advantage.

4.   *The compulsory system of voting.*

Voting is compulsory in Australia, not for the purposes of democracy, but to save the major parties the trouble of getting people to the polling booths. You see, *voting* is not compulsory but *attendance* at a polling booth is. You can always register at the polling booth, take your ballot slip and place it straight in the ballot box (or the garbage bin) without voting at all.

5.   *Political corruption.*

Let us define political corruption as the diversion of public funds or resources to the individual politician where those funds or resources are purely of benefit to the politician, and not necessary as payment for the performance of his or her duties. Outside of the political arena, such diversion is called embezzlement:

   a) *The payment of candidates for each primary vote gained*
   At Federal and State parliamentary levels, a candidate is remunerated for each primary vote he or she gets (presently more than $2.45 per vote). The reasons given for this by the politicians are:

   (i) This prevents major parties being beholden to big business or unions for their funds and therefore decreases the likelihood of corruption of governments. Of course, it does not stop parties accepting money from outside *on top of* the electoral payout. Further, when a candidate stands as a party candidate, the funds go to the party, not to the candidate.

(ii) This allows non-party candidates to be funded and therefore increases the opportunity for more people to stand, which strengthens democracy. But, there is a catch: the minor candidate must poll at least 4% of the total vote of his or her electorate in order to be eligible for the payout. As very few minor candidates reach this 4% quota, very few get any reimbursement and hence the argument is blatant deceit.

Clearly, this system has been instituted to allow the major parties to siphon taxpayers funds to strengthen their own position and to prevent competition from other candidates. At the Federal Election of 2010, the Labor Party collected over $21.2 million and the Liberal/National coalition syphoned off $23.5 million simply for standing candidates. (Who dares to suggest that there is not enough being spent on our health system when there are such overweening demands on the taxpayer's dollar?)

b) *'Living away from home' allowances*
Many politicians use this allowance to buy, or pay off properties (usually in their spouses' names). Of course, politicians are entitled to have reasonable accommodation while serving their electorate and, as one can reasonably argue that the allowance will end up paying off someone's property anyhow, it may as well be that of the politician. If the politicians do not regard this behaviour as tax-avoidance, why do they prohibit people paying off property with superannuation funds and living in those same properties?

c) *Postal allowances for politicians*

Politicians have voted themselves personal postal allowances for electoral purposes that are more than the annual incomes of most people. These allowances are only available to sitting politicians and not to other electoral candidates. This is clearly a diversion of public funds for their personal use designed to give them an unfair advantage over any rivals. Now, with the increased internet usage and very little use of postal services, this really amounts to outright fraud.

Political oppression:

If you believe that your government will only persecute and prosecute 'evil' people, I urge you to think again. Political persecution and malice is all too prevalent in Australia but because it affects so few, there is no general outcry against it. A few examples follow:

1. A foreign doctor is gaoled on a trumped-up charge of supporting terrorists. When the courts order his release, politicians still keep him in custody with no evidence that he is guilty of any crime.

2. A Queensland Magistrate is removed from her office and imprisoned for an alleged abuse of power. On appeal to the High Court, it is declared that she should never have been gaoled as she had legal immunity from the charge. (You might be surprised to learn she was never reinstated because of this injustice.)

3. A media entrepreneur is gaoled for tax evasion after having co-operated with authorities. The usual penalty for tax evasion is to be ordered to pay the unpaid tax and to pay a penalty on top — not a custodial sentence.

These were all acts of pure political bastardry whose

purpose was to instil fear into those who would dare to challenge the powers that be. Where victims of political malice have refused to co-operate with the authorities, they have generally avoided prosecution. Where they have co-operated, they have usually been given much harsher sentences than an average person would have received.

The message seems to be clear: never co-operate or admit guilt because the authorities have been proven to be dishonest and malicious whenever it suited their political agenda. Without co-operation, it is much more difficult for authorities to obtain enough evidence for a conviction.

'Politicians and other scoundrels would sell their mothers for sixpence—the only difference is that Politicians would deliver.'

Anon

10 | DRUGS, GAMBLING AND PROSTITUTION

The great areas of high profits and high wealth creation for little effort are those of *drugs, gambling* and *prostitution*. In all of these, the outlays are minimal or non-existent while the returns are massive.

Drugs

There are a number of illicit drugs available on the streets of our cities. How harmful are these drugs and why are they illicit?

Ask any health professional: 'If you had the choice of making either alcohol or heroin legal and the other illegal, what would you choose?' Without question, alcohol is the more damaging of the two. Alcohol does enormous damage to society as a result of the antisocial acts of those under the influence; it does enormous damage to individuals as a result of its effects on the body. So why is alcohol (and indeed, tobacco) legal? The fact that it generates huge revenues for governments, regardless of its damage to society, might be a clue. The fact that alcohol can also be produced from a wide range of vegetable materials also makes government oversight difficult.

People have simply assumed that drugs must be harmful because the authorities have outlawed them. Certainly drugs can be harmful if used in large quantities over long periods of time, but any dangers of narcotics are entirely confined to the user. If I choose to harm myself, what is that to you?

Over a century ago, when narcotics (Morphine, Laudanum, etc.) were freely available, there were nowhere near the numbers of addicts we see today. There are no reports that any such addicts acted in a dangerous and antisocial manner. In fact, the British originally introduced opium into China for the very purpose of having a malleable and subdued population.

Why are narcotics so expensive when they are dirt cheap to grow? The answer is an interesting example of supply and demand. 'Pushing' drugs would not be worthwhile unless there was a considerable profit margin. As drugs are extremely cheap to produce and bring to market, one has to make them artificially expensive. By illegalising the drugs, the costs can be artificially inflated and the profit margin can thus be artificially expanded. This now makes it worthwhile to push the drugs onto an otherwise disinterested community and provides magnificent profits with minimal effort.

Narcotics are artificially expensive because they are illegal!

Is there any less availability of narcotics because they are proscribed? Is the health of our youth improved by these laws? Anyone on drugs will tell you that they can walk into nearly any town in Australia and obtain pretty much any drug they want within a couple of hours (at a price, of course). Clearly, anti-drug laws have had no effect on the availability of drugs. When I was young, Australia had no such drug problem — the population was too small and the profitability of the drug trade was not worth the effort.

Our drug problem could be solved in six months if drugs were legalised. Without large profits, the drug barons would lose interest and it would be unprofitable to 'push' the drugs. Very few would be interested in trying narcotics just for fun in the same way that very few indulge in petrol-sniffing. And, even if they did, they would simply sit happily in a corner and trouble nobody.

The community danger of drugs is entirely due to the need of the user to gain finance to pay for them. The reality is that drug distribution today could not occur without the support and connivance of governmental authorities and our captains of industry. These are the people who make the large profits. The poor 'mule' who straps a kilo of heroin to their waist and tries to sneak it through customs is right at the bottom of the food chain. If they get caught, gaoled or executed, who cares? The drug barons who promised to pay them $10,000 to carry it through customs lose nothing if the mule is caught. On the next successful run, they will make millions on the streets (minus the $10,000 transport fee) to make up for their regrettable loss. And do you know what? No one will ever be able to point a finger at the drug baron because their financial input will be untraceable.

It is interesting to note that since the US invasion of Afghanistan, the production of opium from that region has ballooned. One does not hear of the US air force napalm bombing the opium fields to protect the world from the evil effects of morphine. With all the cutting-edge electronics that can even distinguish between insurgents and innocent civilians, you would think they would be able to detect hectares of opium poppies from the air, wouldn't you? It is also interesting to note the support of the US for regimes in South America that finance themselves with the cocaine trade. And all of these drugs end up on the streets of America.

The tragedy of illegalising certain drugs is that very valuable agents are denied to the community. Let us look at *marijuana*, otherwise known as *Indian hemp*. Indian hemp grows like a weed in many parts of the world. Its stalks produce an excellent fibre which can make high grade paper — paper of better quality than that produced from wood. Even though the better product could be produced on a large scale and save our forests from destruction, it is illegal to grow! I wonder why? The plant is readily renewable and would save the destruction of millions of trees. So, why are we denied this fibre for the production of paper?

Heroin is a wonderful analgesic – much better than morphine. Half a century ago, it used to be used to great advantage for the relief of the pain of childbirth. It was virtually unheard of for any of these women to become addicted. So why is it now denied to women in childbirth? It is not available for them anymore, but it is freely available for our drug barons to sell on the streets. With a limited supply, one must have priorities.

Gambling and Prostitution

Gambling and prostitution are more high-profit—low-cost operations. This profitability is also enhanced by making them illegal.

As a result of being illegal, profits from prostitution can be magnified by means of a protection-racket approach to the workers involved. The introduction of drugs to the prostitutes increases the number of sex slaves who must continue in order to service their newly acquired habit. With prostitution, the state also has difficulty in extracting its dues. Nowadays, we do have some legalisation of this profession but, again, it is safe to assume that there is somewhat less than full accounting of the profits for tax purposes; better some income than none. Even when it was illegal to live off the earnings of prostitution, governments had no scruples about taking tax money from prostitutes.

There are areas where the government is able to control and tax gambling (e.g. poker machines, registered bookmakers) but it is safe to assume that even these venues do not render unto Caesar that which Caesar would really like to extract.

Drugs, gambling, and prostitution are illegal because it increases profit margins. None of these enterprises would incur damage to innocent people (including murder of some of those involved) if they were not illegal. But, if they were not illegal, the profits would not be as great.

I rest my case.

11 | THE JUSTICE SYSTEM

Laws

All games involving more than one person need rules. Life is no exception. We all accept the need for a standard set of rules so that we know when we are doing the right thing and, especially, when others are not. If the rules and penalties for disobedience apply equally to all, we have very little objection. We call that fair play or justice.

Nevertheless, we need to appreciate that all rules and laws are quite arbitrary even though they set a general code of behaviour that everyone can understand. There is nothing absolutely correct about any law. In Australia, we drive on the left side of the road; in Europe and the United States, they drive on the right. It does not really matter which side one drives on as long as everyone does the same thing. Oft times, we lose sight of the arbitrary nature of rules and customs and tend to believe that certain actions are inherently right or wrong because that is what we have been brought up to believe. We also tacitly accept that all of our laws are fair and that they should be obeyed without question.

Laws, however, are made by the ruling classes and reflect the interests of those classes. Because most people accept order, it is easy for our rulers to impose laws that are of no particular benefit to the individual or to society but are of benefit to them. If you rob a bank, you might get ten years in gaol, but if you scam millions of dollars from old-age pensioners, as a result of some anomaly in the law, you will probably only be accused of being a leech.

Governments at their best tend to be dictatorial; at worst, tyrannical. At the beginning of World War I, the Australian Commonwealth Government introduced the *Commonwealth Crimes Act*.

CRIMES ACT 1914 - SECT 70
Disclosure of information by Commonwealth officers

1. A person who, being a *Commonwealth officer*, publishes or communicates, except to some person to whom he or she is authorised to publish or communicate it, any fact or document which comes to his or her knowledge, or into his or her possession, by virtue of being a *Commonwealth officer*, and which it is his or her duty not to disclose, shall be guilty of an offence.
Penalty: Imprisonment for 2 years

This section is used by politicians to conceal, by the threat of imprisonment, behaviour that would be embarrassing to themselves.

Recently (2005), the Australian government has introduced *Anti-Terrorism laws* ostensibly to protect citizens against terrorism. However, these laws contain provisions that have nothing to do with terrorism and all to do with an arbitrary infringement of personal liberties.

For instance:

1. Any person can be accused of terrorism and arrested without any evidence.

2. The person accused of terrorism loses all normal legal rights such as the right to legal representation and the right to be brought immediately before an open court to challenge the validity of his or her detention. It used to be a basic principle of justice that an accused person shall have the right to face his or her accusers and be able to test all of the evidence against them in an open court. If the accused do not have access to any part of such evidence, how can they test it and prove it to be wrong? What is to stop an accuser simply pretending that there is evidence?

3. Any person observing such an arrest commits a crime if he or she discloses that fact.

Under these laws, a politician can point at anybody, accuse him or her of being a terrorist and then claim that the evidence against them must be kept secret from the court for the 'reasons of national security'. The basic reason for secrecy is to prevent other people finding out what they are up to. The only reason to conceal such affairs from the public is to enable the accusers to pursue their own agenda without interference. It also allows our politicians to do things that the public would be appalled with. Thus, any one of us could find ourselves in gaol for decades without being able to come before a court to prove that an accusation was false. There is a more sinister possibility: under the secrecy provisions of the anti-terrorism law, a person could simply 'disappear' and the authorities could deny any knowledge of his or her whereabouts. If the present laws are obeyed to the letter, there is no way of proving that the authorities were even involved.

Can we trust our politicians to be honest in their accusations against political enemies? Could we rule out the possibility that they would murder opponents if there was no method of proving their involvement? Why do I ask such rhetorical questions? Our rulers have repeatedly shown that they are not to be trusted. Many of Australia's 'security' laws are purely designed to protect the rulers from scrutiny and to intimidate the populace.

Crime

In essence, crime is simply a disobedience of the law. As laws are arbitrary and made by the rulers to suit themselves, it follows that they may not suit anyone else. One therefore needs to examine each law to determine how just or necessary that law is. Where laws are unjust, it can be argued that there is a moral and civic duty to resist them. Where unjust laws are not resisted, further oppression inevitably results. If improper or irrelevant laws were resisted more often, perhaps we would have better and fewer laws.

> *'All that is necessary for the triumph of evil is that good men do nothing.'*
> Edmund Burke (1729–1797)

If we don't agree with the rules, we have two choices:

1. Abide with them and be quiet for the sake of peace.

2. Resist the law but be prepared to accept the consequences.

How many murders or thefts do laws prevent? It is said that, when pick-pocketing was a hanging offence, pickpockets did their best business at the public executions! Laws cannot stop crimes being committed; they can only prescribe punishment if they are.

Where one cannot be sure of the law, the law becomes meaningless and no one can have confidence in it. The general principle is *'that which is not prohibited is permitted.'* This essentially draws a line in the sand — if I stay on this side of the line I am fine, but if I cross that line I could end up in trouble. Unfortunately, this principle is often ignored by lawmakers and others alike:

1. In 1975, Sir John Kerr, the Governor-General of Australia from 1974 to 1977, used his reserve powers under the Constitution to dismiss the Whitlam government. Some sectors of the community (beside Gough Whitlam, the Prime Minister at the time) were outraged by this action. The reality was that John Kerr was legally entitled to do this. If a law is wrong, then change the law but do not complain about someone acting within it.

2. An Australian rugby team went to New Zealand. During the tour, a number of players had sexual relations with a woman in a motel room. The act was apparently consensual at the time although the woman later had regrets. The incident was investigated and no charges were laid. In spite of this, one of the players later lost a TV-contract on the basis that he should not have done this. Here, a person was victimised because of the moral views of some people, even though he was acting within the law. This was not the sort of scenario that many people would engage in, nor is it a scenario that one would wish on one's daughter. But if a law is wrong, then change the law, do not victimise someone who is acting within it.

Laws cannot be perfect and can lead to unintended consequences. Where people are unfairly dealt with because of unintended consequences of the law, our legislators need to have some method of remedying that problem. However, when people are legitimately acting within a law that is deficient, it is unjust to penalise them at a later time by changing the law retrospectively (retrospective legislation).

'Justice not only has to be seen to be done, it has to be seen to be believed.'

Peter Cook (1937–1995)

Although laws were originally meant to embrace the concept of justice, 'law' and 'justice' are not necessarily synonymous. Where the law and justice conflict, the law (the written rules) will always takes precedence. There is a definite logic to this. The law, written or well-known, tends to be clear; justice is a more subjective concept. Thus, 'justice' can be interpreted more broadly even though the law itself is liable to broad interpretation. If laws were always clear and not open to interpretation, we would not need lawyers or judges.

'Rules are made for the guidance of wise men and for the blind obedience of fools.'

Douglas Bader (1910–1982)

The rules of evidence often ensure that the truth is not exposed. If there is evidence that a certain event occurred, why are the courts concerned to ensure that it was obtained 'legally'? One would think that facts are facts no matter who provides them or how they come to the light of day. If facts are obtained illegally, prosecute the person who has broken the law but don't conceal the facts themselves.

Punishment

There are two types of criminals: those who are a danger to society and those who are not. Where a person is dangerous, it makes sense to confine or eliminate them so that society is protected. But it makes no sense to confine those who are not dangerous unless vengeance is the objective.

There are many crimes that present no danger to members of the public. Crimes such as theft (without violence or terrorism) surely would be better dealt with by making the thief repay the cost of his or her theft, perhaps with interest. Accountants who embezzle clients' funds would repay their crime more efficiently by repaying the debt. Furthermore, professionals have a greater capacity to generate income and therefore a greater ability to efficiently repay a debt. When we put them in jail, not only do we lose their skills, they now become a burden on society. If a person steals your television set, of what use is it to you if the miscreant is sent to gaol? Wouldn't it be better if he or she replaced the stolen item? The cost of keeping a criminal in prison is approximately $50,000 per year. You could buy a lot of TV sets for that. In fact, if you paid prisoners $50,000 per year, you could pretty much abolish crime of the non-dangerous kind. There is, of course, the problem that such a scheme would produce a long line of people wishing to become criminals.

There are crimes where the criminal *is* a danger to society. If we are dealing with a person who has committed serial murders or one who has murdered out of uncontrollable rage, surely that person presents a continuing danger to the public. Such criminals need to be confined at least. There is a legal principle known as the 'McNaghten Rules', named after Daniel McNaghten, a Scottish wood-turner, who, in 1843, attempted to assassinate the British Prime Minister but instead killed a public servant. He was found 'not guilty on the ground of insanity', and has given his name to the legal test of *criminal insanity*. McNaghten Rules maintain that a person should not be punished for a crime if they did not know the quality of the crime committed. These rules would seem to be humane but they lack logic: if a person kills and does not regard it as wrong, what is to stop them repeating the offence? Wouldn't such a person be the most dangerous person to have loose on our streets?

If there is a mad dog roaming the streets, the animal is captured and 'put down'. This is not because the dog acted in a premeditated manner, or because it knew that what it did was wrong. There is no fanfare or malice in this act — it is purely a logical way to ensure that the animal presents no further danger to the community. Why is it unreasonable to deal with dangerous murderers in the same manner as the mad dogs, and with the same humanity and lack of cruelty? It is said that the death penalty is not a deterrent, but to my knowledge, no executed murderer has ever repeated the crime. The underlying fear of opponents of capital punishment is that they, personally, might accidentally end up on the end of a rope. This is the real driver of the anti-hanging debate, not the logic of safety for the public or even the justice of proper punishment for a crime.

On the other hand, there are people who take the lives of others and are not a danger to society. Consider the husband who takes the life of his beloved wife—to whom he has been married for over fifty years—to relieve her incurable pain. Is he a danger to the society, or is he likely to repeat the offence?

If a crime is committed, the punishment should fit the crime. If we *add* to prescribed punishment in order to deter others, we are punishing him or her for a crime they did not commit. The punishment being increased as a deterrent is a method of adding fear to the mind of the average citizen. It is therefore a mechanism of control and not justice.

Prisons

'The yokel mind loves stories from of old
Being the kind it can repeat and hold.'
Geoffrey Chaucer (1343–1400)

All countries have prisons. For everyone alive today, there have always been prisons. Prisons do not invade our consciousness on a daily basis. The fact that they have always been there leads us to accept that they are an integral part of our society and that they are therefore necessary. We accept the word of authority without question: if they say we need prisons, we must need them. But do we? Of what social use are they really?

Where did the habit of imprisonment arise? If we go back in history, we find that the deprivation of liberty was a method used by the rulers to enforce compliance with their wishes. If a peasant stole something from a Baron or displeased him in some other way, the peasant was incarcerated as a punishment to the peasant himself and also as an example to others. The clear message was: 'Don't screw around with the Baron.'

We pretend that prisons are there to *rehabilitate* prisoners. How can one make person a good member of society by isolating them from society? How many people learn to drive a car by being confined to the back seat?

The currency in prisons is violence. Assault, standover tactics and sodomy are common. But what do the authorities do to eliminate these crimes and protect prisoners from them? Is this what the authorities call 'rehabilitation'? Prisons do not rehabilitate or increase the ability of prisoners to become better citizens. They are not even safe places for prisoners. The authorities do not even insist on a basic level of lawful behaviour or decent conduct in prisons. Our authorities are building more gaols and incarcerating more people every year. The fact that increasing numbers of people are being gaoled each year shows that our present justice system is not an effective anti-crime measure. Imprisonment is only an act of vengeance and it constitutes a breeding ground for more crime.

We also talk of the prisoners having to 'repay their debt to society'. Have I missed something here? If there is a debt, to whom does this prisoner really owe it? Here we have a person who, let's say, has stolen a television set. We then go through the lengthy and expensive process of a trial and eventually, we send them to gaol. When they are imprisoned, we house them, feed them and pay wardens to ensure they stay there. And who is paying for all this? Society is, not the prisoner! So our criminal effectively pays nothing to the person to whom they really owe the debt (the owner of the TV), and society, which had nothing to do with the whole shemozzle, pays the bill for the prisoner's upkeep. Would we not be better off by leaving the television thief free but requiring them to replace the stolen goods?

It is expedient for politicians to pretend they are tough on crime and that they are doing something about it. But crime also has causes such as poverty or inability to improve one's standard of living. These causes are not being addressed by our politicians. And people who have served prison terms are returned to the same environment that caused the initial problem. Now, not only have they returned to a poor environment but they are back with the added burden of a gaol sentence, just to make sure that they will never be able to rehabilitate themselves.

Our authorities need prisons to instil fear into the populace. In order to be afraid of going to prison, one must have prisons of which to be afraid. If we consider the huge expense to society and the waste of a prisoner's (and the warden's) life, we must conclude that fear and vengeance are very important to our rulers.

Prisons are not instruments of justice and rehabilitation; they are instruments of blackmail, vengeance and consolidation of state power.

12 | EDUCATION

The French philosopher Michel de Montaigne (1533–1592), maintained that much education consisted of teaching knowledge rather than wisdom. In this respect, he categorised 'knowledge' as fact, but 'wisdom' as the ability to understand and use those facts. Even though we have had some four centuries to heed his advice, our education system today has not advanced beyond the state that existed in his day.

We rarely teach our children how to use the information they acquire. We instil rules and customs without explaining the *reasons* for such things. If you know what your goal is, you can work out many different methods to arrive at that goal. If you do not know what the purpose of your learning is, you will not know how or when to apply it.

We wonder why so many young people die on our roads. The rate of road deaths of those under 25 is about double that of those over 25. Because children have rules and restrictions imposed upon them for no apparent reason, they later tend to rebel against what they regard as tyranny without purpose. When they get to drive a car by themselves, they are now freed from this tyranny and are able to do as they like. They do not realise that the road rules are designed to protect rather than tyrannise them because no one has bothered to tell them. Hence, they deliberately disobey the rules with the common consequence of injury or death. Teaching young people the mechanics of driving without teaching them how and why to drive carefully is like teaching someone how to shoot a gun without teaching him how to use it safely.

Schools and the education system did not originate to teach students to think or to understand. They began as parish schools to inculcate religion. If you only want children to believe what they are taught, debate is a big disadvantage. This historical system of teaching remains today, so we have an adversarial system of education. Education becomes a system of hurdles to be conquered, while the teachers are viewed by the student as obstacles rather than allies.

Teachers have a tendency to believe that their methods of teaching are efficient. Therefore, if the student does not understand, then it must be the student's fault. Teachers rarely invest any effort to ensure that their students understand what they are taught. Nor is any significant effort applied to auditing the quality and efficiency of the teaching. In short, there is no *quality control.*

Quality control has been understood and applied in industrial fields for decades. Let us look at an industrial production control system, for example, for the production of ball-bearings. First, the production line is designed to produce ball-bearings of a given size and quality. This line is then set into motion and a test-run are initiated. A sample from this test-run is tested for size and quality. If less than a certain percentage (say 97.5%) meets the specifications, the production line will be fine-tuned until the required percentage is achieved.

The flow chart for this process is as follows:

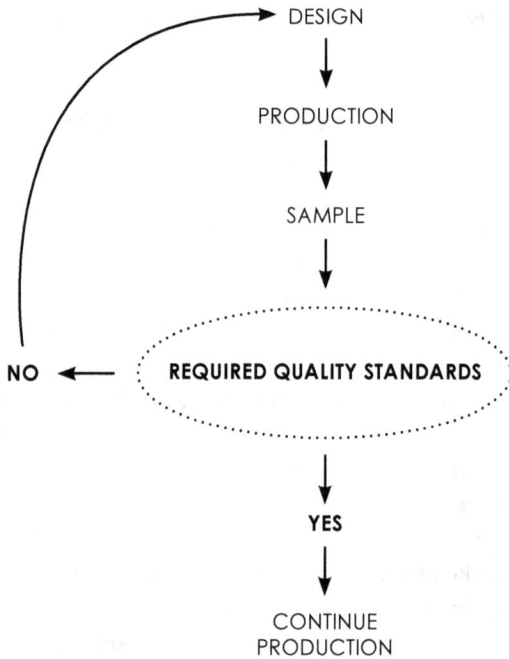

```
                           DESIGN
                             │
                             ▼
                        PRODUCTION
                             │
                             ▼
                          SAMPLE
                             │
                             ▼
NO  ◄──  ⟨ REQUIRED QUALITY STANDARDS ⟩
                             │
                             ▼
                            YES
                             │
                             ▼
                        CONTINUE
                       PRODUCTION
```

In respect to education, the previous diagram could be modified as follows:

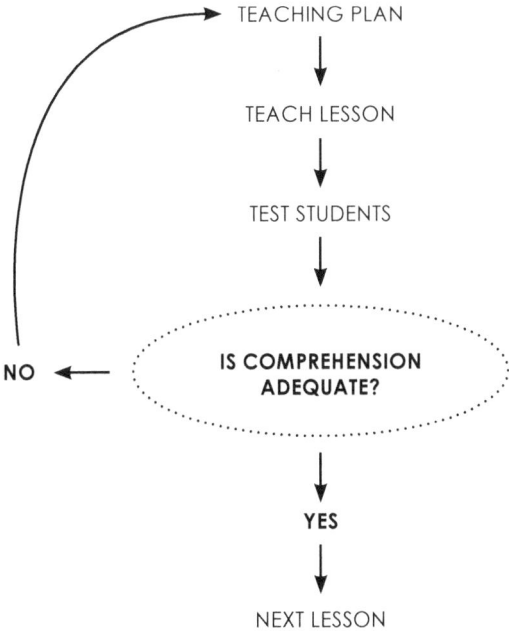

Unfortunately, the above quality control algorithm is rarely followed.

This is what generally occurs:

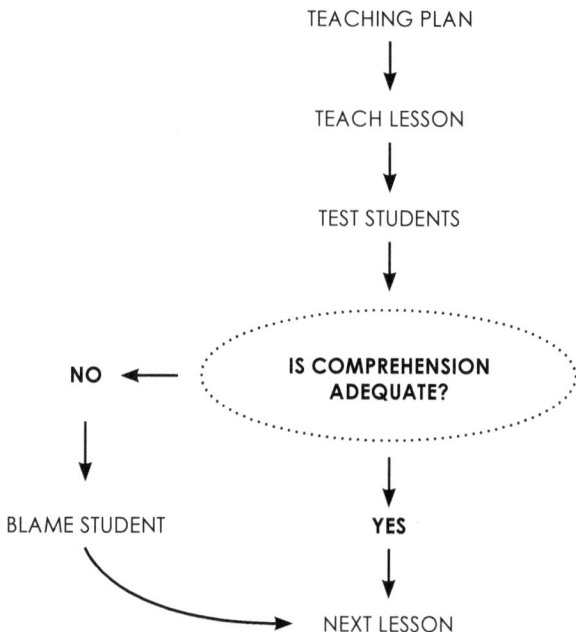

```
                    TEACHING PLAN
                          |
                          v
                    TEACH LESSON
                          |
                          v
                    TEST STUDENTS
                          |
                          v
   NO  <-----  ( IS COMPREHENSION
                    ADEQUATE?     )
    |
    |                     |
    v                     v
BLAME STUDENT            YES
    \                     |
     \                    v
      ------------>  NEXT LESSON
```

After students are lectured, they are examined on what they know. If they know enough — good; if they don't — bad luck. Tests never seem to be used by teachers as a feedback mechanism to let them know what they have, or have not managed to convey to the student.

If we hope to teach students efficiently, we need to adopt an algorithm as above – but not the one *immediately* above!

The following teaching procedures need to be instituted:

1.   Set down precisely and in detail what knowledge is required.
2.   Teach that knowledge in a manner that ensures that the students assimilate it.
3.   Test the knowledge to see that the students have absorbed the required information.
4.   On the basis of any deficiencies revealed by the test, re-teach the information that has not been absorbed to ensure that the students have learned it.

This process would also help teachers to determine what information they were teaching effectively and what information they were not imparting too well. As students vary in their ability to absorb information, some pieces of knowledge may not be learnt by some students but be easily absorbed by others. Thus, individual tuition is also necessary. But teachers will also find that sometimes the information they try to impart does not get through to most students. In this case, teachers are at fault and need to modify their teaching method or go into more detail to provide a satisfactory explanation that can be understood by all students.

We place very little emphasis on the subjects that people really need in order to be safe and to do well in life. Such subjects include law, finance, health and motor-vehicle driving. We continue to place great emphasis on those subjects that have been taught historically. We need to use our education system to provide our students with knowledge useful in the modern world rather than something to fill in their time until they start work.

Knowledge is an interesting thing. Once acquired, it cannot be lost or stolen. If you leave your child a legacy of knowledge, he or she cannot blow it in one afternoon at the horse races. There are only two things you can do with knowledge — you can either use it or pass it on. And, do you know what? Knowledge is the only thing you can give away and still have as much left as when you started.

Another problem with our adversarial attitude is that teachers tend to feel that students should not excel them. A moment's thought should tell us that this attitude is crazy. If the master is any good, the student should always excel them because the student is starting from where the master left off and can only get better. How long did it take Kepler to formulate his rules of planetary motion? And how long does it take now to learn those rules and apply them? We are not smarter than Kepler, but we certainly know more. This is the inexorable progress of civilisation. We are smarter than our parents and our children will, of necessity, be smarter than us. This is not to be decried but to be celebrated. If our children do not end up better than us, then we have failed.

We all fear failure. We fear that failure will prove that we, unlike others, cannot cope. But what is failure?

Failure merely means that we have not done something right. There is nothing to be learned from success because success means that you have achieved the correct goal. The only way we can learn is by making mistakes and learning from them. If we do not learn from our failures, we have wasted a golden opportunity delivered to us by fate.

'The person who doesn't make mistakes is unlikely to make anything. Failures and false starts are a precondition of success.'
Paul Arden (1940–2008)

When you do not succeed, first examine why. Then use that knowledge to succeed the next time. When you watch a professional tennis player, you are, no doubt, amazed at how skilfully they hit the ball over the net to exact place they intend the ball to go. Have you ever asked yourself how many times they hit the ball into the net before they acquired that skill? I'll bet they have hit it into the net more times than you ever will!

The trouble with our teaching regime is that we present students with much information but we do not teach them how to absorb it efficiently. Students, therefore, do not know how to learn and they do not know when they have learned what is required.

How to study

The purpose of study is to memorise information.

There is an efficient process of memorisation. Information is absorbed into the brain where it is correlated and stored. At a later time, we wish to access this information in order to use it.

Information input ➝ **Memory storage** ➝ Information output

Contrary to a popular belief, the stage of memory storage is very efficient. When someone states that he or she has a poor memory, it is not that they do not retain the information, but that they are unable to *recall* the information that has already been stored.

Storage and recall of memory information is done by *association* — an idea or concept is linked to another idea or concept that has already been memorised. Thus, to recall information, we must have some trigger that will link us to the information we wish to recall. If we do not create such a link, we will probably be unable to evoke the information we want. If we simply read an article without such organisation, our memory bank is like a shoe-box filing system. In such a system, files are just thrown willy-nilly into a big box. So if we want to retrieve ideas from a similarly organised mind, we are unlikely to do so efficiently, if at all. But if we store our ideas logically, we will be able to recall those ideas more readily at a later time.

There are two main memory systems used by the experts: the *peg system* and the *chain system*:

1. The Peg system
In this system, one has a series of memory pegs, each peg usually being a consonant letter associated with a number. For example, the number 1 might be associated with the letter T, the number 2 with the letter N, and the number 3 with the letter M. (Note the vertical strokes in these letters happen to equal the number as an extra aid to memory.) In this system, we also could visualise T as a teacup, N as a neck and M as a monster. If we now want to memorise a shopping list of, say, clothes pegs, eggs and salami, we might create an association of a teacup full of clothes pegs, egg yolk all over our necks and a monster chewing large salami. One can buy books on such systems or invent one's own.

2. The Chain System
In this system, one idea is linked to the next. This might be on a time basis, a geographical basis or use any other system that suits the circumstances.

For exam purposes, one needs to consider the type of question-triggers that might stimulate recall of the above memory sequences

How to study reading material

1. On first reading, *rapidly* read the chapter. The idea is to get an overall picture and appreciation of the material. Re-read the material. This time, be sure to understand all of it and clarify any confusing points.

2. Make notes, in a point form, of the material. Simply note each point as it comes up and perhaps underline points that you feel are particularly important. Rearrange the points that you have written down into a sequence that is logical and easy to follow in your own mind.

3. Memorise these points using one of the above memorisation techniques. Make strong visual associations between the points and the types of question you might imagine an examiner will ask.

4. Now take a break for an hour (or move on to other work).

5. After the break, go over the points you have memorised without looking at your notes. Where you find gaps or haziness in the recalled information, revisit those points and reinforce the memorisation with stronger visualisation techniques.

6. The following day, revisit the material without looking at your notes and repeat any reinforcement as necessary.

It is important to follow the above routine in its entirety.

It is tempting to think that you can take a short cut by omitting one of the revisits to the information. If you do not revisit the information in the early stages, you will later waste many hours trying to re-learn information that you could have got under your belt with a few minutes revision in the first place.

Keep your notes (preferably in a card file) for revision before the exams. Revisit your information and ensure that it remains clear in your mind. Reinforce any hazy bits. When you enter the exam room you will be quite confident that you have all the information needed to pass if you follow these instructions.

By using the above systems, a student will know that they have covered all of the material, sufficiently memorised that material and, what is more, he or she will *know* that they know the material.

Learning material for exams, therefore, consists of acquiring information, remembering it and later recalling it.

There is no crime in *being* ignorant — the crime is in *staying* ignorant.

13 | HEALTH

In about 1966 or 1967, the editor of Melbourne's *Age* newspaper, Mr Graham Perkin, ran a series of three articles called *'Medicine in the Market Place'*. These articles queried the dedication of doctors to treatment of patients rather than acquisition of income. This was the beginning of a propaganda onslaught that resulted in the introduction of the *Health Insurance Act* 1973, otherwise known as the *Medibank Act*.

If its purpose was to limit the income of doctors, Medibank failed spectacularly. Most doctors tripled their incomes within two years. Doctors were soon buying Rolls Royces at a prodigious rate and overseas trips were the order of the day. (One day, I noted a consultant doctor arriving at the hospital in a moderate Ford car. When I asked what had become of his Rolls Royce, he told me that he had sold it because he was fed up with being abused by people he didn't even know.)

The introduction of Medibank was poorly thought out. Doctors warned the government against it due to its likely problems. The government response was that doctors were 'greedy bastards' and went ahead anyhow. The problems outlined by doctors all came to pass, and naturally, the doctors were blamed for them. The outcome was that doctors ceased giving suggestions as to how the service might be improved (not that they were ever encouraged to do so). The attitude of the profession became: 'Okay, you do it your way and we'll look after ourselves.'

For political reasons, this Act was designed to break the 'doctor–patient' relationship in the treatment of patients in public hospitals. As a result, doctors were removed from having any input into the medical requirements of patients. This meant that the funding and decisions regarding necessary facilities were assigned to bureaucrats rather than those who knew what was required. It is also of note that those bureaucrats are often assigned on the basis of political loyalty rather than on the basis of any expertise.

A healthy dislike of doctors seems to be a prime prerequisite for such bureaucratic appointment. As a result of such a system, those organising health care and those delivering it do not speak to one another. Because of this schism between administrators and medical personnel, the bureaucrats managing the health system have little idea what they are doing. This results in fudging of budgets and the concealment of unpleasant truths from both the community and government.

Our present system is heavily overloaded with bureaucrats. We have unit managers, district managers, cluster managers, etc., but very few people actually treating sick people. Hence, when a government trumpets its increased allotment of finance to health care, what it is really doing is transferring an increased amount of taxpayers' money to the pockets of its chosen bureaucrats. No real increase in funding finds its way to health needs or patient care.

Further to this, politicians have introduced a

system of regional management of the hospital system. Regional management does have its advantages but it has mostly become a device to shift responsibility from government to administrators.

As the costs of the 'free' health system began to blow the government's budget, funding for hospitals tightened. As funding to hospitals decreased, hospital managers went to health ministers complaining that they could not run the hospitals on the money they were given. The response was typically bureaucratic: 'Well, if you can't run the hospital on the funds we give you, we'll find someone who can.'

So now we had a situation where hospital managers had a choice: either work within the budget or lose your job! Surprisingly, managers, almost to a man, chose the first alternative.

In order to work within budget, managers extended the usual Christmas closing period of the operating theatres from one to about four weeks. That, of course, saved money, but guess what it did to surgical waiting lists? Long waiting lists are politically uncomfortable, so, as elections approach, governments make a great song and dance about decreasing them – and the inefficient way they go about it costs the taxpayer plenty.

So the circus goes on. Theatres close, waiting lists expand, doctors get paid a premium to reduce the lists, and so *ad infinitum*. But I'm a doctor, so don't think I am ungrateful. Unfortunately, I also see the affects on patients first-hand. Let me tell you that those 'thousand hip replacements' on a statistic sheet mean nothing compared to one patient sitting across your desk with pain engraved on their face asking for an explanation why they have to wait two years for their 'free' medical treatment.

There is a simple way to correct the hospital funding problem, but politicians would be unlikely to accept it as it would bring their hypocrisy into stark relief.

An independent audit of each hospital needs to be done according to the following guidelines:

1. What services *is* this hospital providing?
2. What services *should* this hospital provide?
3. What services is this hospital providing that it *should not* be providing?
4. What personnel (doctors, nurses, administrators, ancillary staff) is required to provide the services that the hospital should be providing?
5. What facilities (buildings, equipment) are required to service the above needs of the hospital?

Estimate the cost of the above — *that is the funding required.*

If a minister refuses to provide the funds required, they simply need to be asked to define the elements they are not prepared to fund, so that the hospital managers can tell the press and the public: 'These are the community needs the minister refuses to fund'.

The medical profession must take responsibility for part of this debacle. In fairness, the reaction of the profession was logical and predictable. The profession simply left the entire management to the bureaucrats and didn't waste any further time trying to give advice.

Another medical factor which has come into play is the increase in numbers of doctors who wish to train as specialists. The reaction of the colleges has been to try to minimise these numbers in order to guarantee employment and income to those already working within the specialties. This has led to prolonged and poor training of all candidates. In the 1960's one could become a qualified surgeon within four post-graduate years. Now it can take up to 10-15 years to achieve the same result.

Government response to the deficit in numbers of trained doctors has been to increase the intake to medical colleges and to import foreign graduates. The glut of doctors thus created is about to hit the market – with a likely result somewhat akin to the proverbial material hitting the fan.

The government has made the same blunder with the training of nurses with states like Queensland having up to 90% of new nursing graduates without a job.

14 | SCIENCE

Scientists are not immune from old dogmas either. They are not prepared to concede that the universe was created by some supernatural being. So they dream up a hypothesis that still concedes that every effect must have a cause: the 'big bang theory'. This theory postulates that there was originally one speck of matter of infinitesimal size and enormous mass. This speck, for unknown reasons and without any intelligence directing it, suddenly decided to explode and thus created time and space.

Now, what is the difference between the big bang theory and the original creation myth? In both, there is the sudden creation of something out of nothing. Philosophically, there is no difference in the arguments. In the creation myth, there is an intelligent creator; in the 'big bang' theory, the creation simply happened without an intelligent cause. Both theories ignore the *why* and *how* of creation. Both theories fail to explain what existed before our known universe. They both fail to explain how God or the initial mass came into existence in the first place.

The 20th century must surely go down in history as the century of failed scientific theories. We have the failures of Marx and perhaps the child-rearing ideas of Dr Spock (although, in fairness, much ascribed to Spock was not enunciated by him). The 21st century is starting off pretty much on the same tack with the failure of theories of climate change.

At the beginning of the 20th century, Albert Einstein (1879–1955) captivated the scientific world with his *Special* and *General Theories of Relativity*. Even though he made postulates that have never been proved, a large industry has now developed to investigate these postulates. Because so much money is now involved, the scientific world has no interest in publishing any facts that might prove that Einstein was wrong. We even come across mind-boggling statements like 'such and such cannot occur because that would be contrary to Einstein's Theory of Relativity'. In other words, if nature does something that contradicts Einstein, then nature is wrong!

The Theory of Relativity is nothing more than a restatement of a concept that has been obvious for centuries – namely, that your perception of reality depends on where you stand in relation to it. Over the years, scientists have tried to make their observations *objective* so that reality will be the same to all observers once corrections have been made for observer error and difference in vantage point.

Every first-year physics student learns the importance of observer error and the need to calibrate instruments. But Einstein is above all this. To Einstein, the observer *is* always right no matter how absurd his conclusion, and instruments never need to be calibrated because they are always right. There is never any suggestion of the possibility of observer error or inaccuracy of instruments in either Einstein's Special or General Theories of Relativity.

Feynman stated that you can often be proven wrong but you can never prove that you are right. It followed from this that scientists should spend most of their time looking for evidence to contradict their theories rather than seeking evidence to support it. Regrettably, scientists don't do this. In many cases, scientific theories are easily disproved but the originators and their followers choose to ignore the obvious.

Virtually every postulate of Einstein's theories of relativity has obvious proofs of its fallacy.

> *'Where ignorance is bliss, 'tis folly to be wise.'*
> *Thomas Gray (1716-1771)*

So how should we analyse new theories?

1. When a new theory comes along, we need to immediately ask ourselves whether this is something we *want* to believe. We all want to believe that we will ultimately be able to travel in time. We all *want* to believe that what we observe is always right. We all want to believe that we can get accurate measurements without the irritation of painstakingly calibrating our instruments. All of these factors make the theory of relativity very enticing and lower our powers of critical examination.

2. If a theory is correct, what must logically follow from the premises of the theory? If the results are impossible, the theory cannot be correct. Most of the above criticisms of the Theory of Relativity are based on this method of logic. What Einstein called 'thought experiments,' the rest of us would call 'fantasies.' There is nothing wrong with fantasising because fantasies may ultimately be converted into reality. But when the fantasies are themselves impossible (e.g. an observer 'observing' a beam of light passing away from them), we really must draw the line.

3. Are there any other possible explanations for the phenomena that the theory purports to explain? This is the requirement called 'negative control': if there are other possible explanations for the phenomenon, we cannot just assume that our explanation is the correct one. We must determine all possible causes for the phenomenon that we observed and test each one. We cannot ignore something simply because it goes against the theory we want to believe.

The lack of application of 'negative control' is probably the most common reason why incorrect hypotheses become accepted. Virtually all of the 'proofs' of Einstein's theories fail because they lack this element of negative control.

With any hypothesis, one must first assume that it is wrong and determine other explanations that fit the observations. The danger of accepting a hypothesis and then looking for evidence to support it is shown with the following well-known example:

Hypothesis: *The Earth is the centre of the universe.*

Proof:
1. The Sun orbits the Earth once each day.
2. The Moon orbits the Earth once each day.
3. All of the stars orbit the Earth about once each day.
4. As every extra-terrestrial heavenly body orbits the Earth, the Earth must be the centre of the Universe.

Of course, once one looks for other explanations and evidence against the above proof, the initial hypothesis is easily disproven.

Peer Review is Censorship

If you send discussions such as the one above to the scientific journals, they won't be published. The excuses vary: 'Sorry, this is not our particular line of expertise', or: 'Sorry, we only publish experimental data', etc. For those who claim to be searchers after the truth and promoters of ideas, it is surprising that they fulfil neither of these objectives. Why?

Scientific journals have now adopted a practice known as 'peer review'. With peer review, self-appointed guardians of the "true" knowledge look at a submitted article and decide whether it is fit for other people to read. On the surface, this appears to be commendable. Nobody wants rubbish promulgated as science. But how do these experts decide what is a good science? When one further considers that the people reading a particular learned journal are usually experts in their own right, by what authority does one 'expert' decide that another shall not be permitted to read novel information?

As mentioned earlier, there is now an Einstein industry. Thousands of researchers must be dependent upon it for their daily bread and countless millions of dollars of taxpayers' money are devoted to it. So it is probably not surprising that the scientific journals would refuse to print material that is contrary to the beliefs of the editors. I guess the Vatican journal would probably sidestep the printing of any material that actually proved that God did not exist.

Virtually every advance in scientific knowledge has been against the accepted dogma. One can imagine what would have happened if Martin Luther had submitted his views to Rome for peer review before publishing them. Today's scientists are not going to fall for that one again. The censorship of peer review is therefore vital.

One of the great present day appeals to regard peer

review as valid is in regard to climate change. Where people oppose the view that the climate change fear-mongers wish to present, the dissent is belittled as not being published in peer-reviewed journals. Of course it will not be published in such journals because those controlling the journals do not want such views aired. And the reason they don't want dissident views aired is that the fear-mongering views do not stand up to logical scrutiny.

Because of this censorship, there is probably much information of a great importance that will never reach those who could really use it. With the availability and freedom of the Internet, these censorship barriers are gradually being broken down.

Genetic Engineering

We presently have great debate about genetic engineering and cloning. People are very worried about genetically-modified foods on the basis that they may transmit some lethal virus. Providing the engineering only uses genes from foods we already eat, it seems unlikely that such thing may occur. The reason is that all foods we eat are presently broken down to simpler substances in our gut before they are absorbed into our bodies. Recently, a spinach gene was spliced into a pig cell to increase the nutritional value of the pork. In such a case, the spinach gene can do no harm because it can only create proteins, carbohydrates of fats that would normally occur in spinach. Such genes do not create weird viruses. As a rule, genetic engineering will only result in the production of molecules that we would normally eat. Such molecules may not normally occur in the particular foods that we now find them in but they are not substances foreign to us.

However, this does not remove the need to ensure that genetically-modified foods are safe for consumption before allowing them on the open market.

Cloning also presents an 'ethical' problem. It seems acceptable to clone animals but not humans. On what basis do we make the assumption that human life is somehow superior to any other life form? Again, it comes back to what we are taught to believe. We are told that God made man in his image and gave him dominion over the birds in the air and the beasts in the field. Now, where is the evidence for that? This is simply what we *want* to believe.

We are also presented with the argument that the *chemistry of life is God's domain and an area in which it is improper for us to delve.* There are two arguments against that proposition:

1. God could very easily stop us if He didn't want us to investigate His territory.

2. This argument has been used before and found to be absurd. Before the middle of the 19th century, biochemistry was regarded as something which was not to be meddled with. However, the scientists persevered and brought us many of the miracles of modern medicine. We now have a multitude of drugs, many of which are synthetic, to prevent death and to make life more comfortable. No one today would seriously say that God did not mean for us to have these advantages nor would anyone suggest that we should abandon all these marvellous discoveries.

We need cloning and genetic engineering to advance the security of all life forms on earth. We need these skills to engineer the demise of life-threatening abnormalities and to create new tissues to repair those tissues that we are unable to repair at present.

There is concern that scientists might create a 'master race' by cloning or genetic engineering. So what is the problem? Are today's humans so perfect that they need no improvement? Such engineering will only short-circuit the gradual advancement that mutations and selective breeding are doing at present.

15 | BANKS AND THE ECONOMY

In days gone by, when someone acquired a bit of coinage and did not need to spend it immediately, they tended to hide it under their mattress (which was about the only place one had to hide things in those days). However, such hiding places were not the most secure and individuals sought a safer repository. The local goldsmith became such a place and people would leave their gold coins in the goldsmith's safe care in return for a receipt, which was of no value to any thief. It soon became common knowledge that the goldsmiths kept such coins for safe-keeping and it was not long before people realised that it was possible to borrow money from them. They, of course, charged a small fee (interest) for their services which, like today, was regarded as worth the value of the service.

It was not long before goldsmiths realised that people did not redeem their deposits all that often, so they found that they could safely lend two or more gold coins for each coin deposited. And each coin lent attracted interest.

Present day banks perpetuate the same philosophy as our mediaeval goldsmith. Banks receive money from depositors and pay interest on this money. They then lend out money at a higher rate than they are paying for it. Most people think that banks make their profit from this exchange, but this is only part of the story. Because people do not redeem their deposits frequently, banks can lend more money than they actually have on deposit. In fact, there is no limit to how much they can lend but a ratio of about 10:1 is nowadays regarded as 'prudent lending'. That means that they could lend $10 for every $1 they had on deposit. This is also known as 'fractional lending'.

Let us say that a bank has $100 on deposit and pays 5% interest to the depositor. The cost of borrowing to the bank is therefore $5 per year. But if the bank now lends out $1000 (on the above 10:1 ratio) at 7%, they receive $70 per year as income. This is not a bad profit when the money is not even their own. And that is not all: the bank also expects the borrower to repay the full $1000 originally lent. The bank has to pay back the $100 it originally borrowed from its depositor, but what about the other $900 which had no more financial substance than a ledger entry? Well, they usually give you about twenty-five years to pay that back, so what are you whingeing about? This should make any unfortunate who has lost their house—because they could not make the repayments—feel much better.

How do the banks manage to perpetuate this fiction? All one needs is faith and trust. As long as everyone accepts the validity of a bank cheque, it does not matter if the bank has any value in its vaults. If you present a cheque from bank ABC to your bank, and end up with a deposit in your account, what do you care?

Some years ago, a group of us used to meet for a monthly game of cards. We used to bet about one cent per trick so the school remained under the police radar. At one time, one of our numbers was running short of small change so he wrote a cheque for one dollar which he put into the kitty. Each night, one of us would end up with this cheque and it kept being passed around for about a year. At last, someone got fed up with this and took it to the bank to cash it. You guessed it — it bounced! But we had all enjoyed one year of convivial card-playing while we still had faith in it.

Since banks can lend more money than they have on deposit, they are able to inject money into the economy over and above that printed by the government. Banks can do this because they have a license – a license, in fact, to print money. The problem of inflation can therefore be compounded by the action of banks (inflation being a process in which too much money chases too few goods). What if bank depositors all decided to remove their money at same time – a phenomenon known as 'a run on the bank'? The bank, which has lent $10 for every dollar on deposit, would not be able to honour its obligations and must certainly fail (unless it can obtain the necessary finance from government or fellow banks). This is why the most banks collapsed during the Great Depression of the 1930s and why some big US financial institutions repeated the exercise recently. The recent melt-down in US markets occurred because financial institutions were lending grossly in excess of the prudent ratio, often forty or fifty times their deposit rate.

Regrettably, the Australian government is taking the same view as the American bankers by extending the First Home Owner Grants to people who might be unable to repay them. It is one thing to inject money into an economy to stimulate it. However, it is quite another to lend it to people who are very likely to lose their jobs and then be unable to repay the remainder of their loan. Those affected are therefore likely to lose their cherished homes that they thought were safe and government guaranteed. Of course, like the irresponsible American bankers, the problem of dealing with this scenario will fall to some future government and the cost to some future taxpayers.

Presently, our banks tell us they cannot afford to lower interest rates because of the cost they incur in borrowing to maintain their reserves. Why are banks allowed to create profits and money out of thin air? If such profits can be made so easily, why are banks not nationalised so that the rewards accrue to those who are creating the wealth — the borrowers and taxpayers of the nation rather than the parasitic entrepreneurs? If the government owned the banks, there would be no need for reserves and hence no cost in borrowing to maintain them, nor would there be any need for governments to guarantee bank deposits. People would surely have as much trust in the government itself as they do in any government guarantee.

The problem with nationalisation is that politicians sometimes fail to maintain the high ethical standards we believe they have. Governments, therefore, tend to hive profitable enterprises to their mates or party donors. For the same reasons, governments are reticent to nationalise profitable enterprises even when it is in the public interest. The excuse used is that a government should not compete with private enterprise. This is inarguable as governments have consistently demonstrated their incompetence at any form of management.

There are no real penalties for political negligence. The best that can be done is to remove a party from power. This, however, is only a short-term fix as the same party with the same policies will inevitably return to power within a few years. The danger of removing a negligent government is that its alternative now gets an immediate license to practise even greater excesses.

We have all heard of a 'government budget deficit'. That means the government plans to borrow money to pay for some of its services. Who does the government borrow the money from? Obviously from the lending institutions and the public – to whom it pays interest. A budget deficit financed in this way therefore puts a noose around the neck of the future generations and saddles them with an unnecessarily high interest burden.

If the government owned the bank, it would not have to pay interest on its own borrowings and it would make profits into the bargain.

Economic depression and John Maynard Keynes

One of the most talked about and least understood economists must be John Maynard Keynes (1883–1946). Keynes was a British economist during the Great Depression of the 1930s. He wrote a book called *The General Theory of Employment, Interest and Money*, in which he explained the 'multiplier effect'.

The multiplier effect was not Keynes's invention, but he popularised it. The gist of this effect is as follows:

If a country's economy is contracting (i.e. production and employment are decreasing), one way of fixing this problem is to inject money into that economy. As more money enters the economy, the greedy entrepreneurs cannot wait to get their grubby little hands on it. But to do this, they have to produce more and this requires hiring more labour. More labour means more paid workers who will tend to spend the money they earn. This injects more money into the economy and the process snowballs. Consequently, we get more money leading to more employment leading to more money, etc. We thus have a result in which a small injection of money leads to a multiplier effect on both employment and the supply of circulating money. A depressed economy thereby becomes reinflated. The obvious agent to inject money into an economy is the government.

Based on this principle, economists today are urging the government to spend more. These economists unfortunately do not understand the underlying mechanism of the multiplier effect.

'There are two types of Economist: Those who don't know
and those who don't know they don't know.'

Anon

We need to understand the differences between the British economy of the 1930s and the Australian economy of today:

1. In the 1930s British tax rates were low because the government derived much of its revenue from its overseas dominions. Thus, the government had a store of finance which was somewhat independent of the British financial system generally. If we consider the British financial system as a balloon that was deflating, we can see that an injection of independent government money would help to blow it up again. In Australia today, virtually all of the government money has been taken from within the economy in the first place. For this reason, the result of present-day government spending is like sucking air out of a balloon and believing you re-inflate the balloon by injecting the same air back in.

2. Today, we have computers and robots. If employers have access to more money, they will be more likely to spend it on mechanisation in order to decrease their dependence on labour. The government's tax on employment, known as 'payroll tax', is an added incentive on employers to shed labour. There is no payroll tax on robots, nor do they require superannuation, sick pay or redundancy pay, and what is more, you get a tax deduction and no squealing when you throw them on the scrap heap and replace them.

3. The level of personal debt is high today where it was low in the 1930s. Accordingly, when people today get money and think of hard times ahead, they are more likely to use it to decrease personal debt rather than putting it back into the general economy by buying consumer goods.

So, what can the government do to avoid a *depression*? The following points are just some of the possibilities out of many. I make no recommendations; I merely advance a few suggestions – and warnings:

1. It can borrow more money.
2. It can print more money.
3. It can spend money on labour intensive industries.
4. It can start major development programs.
5. It can start a war.

Starting a war has many advantages for the government: fixed wages, production of short-lived materials such as bombs can be expanded, etc. It does decrease unemployment — some of it permanently. War, of course, has some major disadvantages, but this has never been a political deterrent. The disadvantages accrue to people other than those making money out of it.

Globalisation

Globalisation is another economic entity that deserves some scrutiny. The idea is that if the markets of all nations are open and free, then countries that can make a particular item most efficiently and cheaply will do so, while other nations that cannot produce the item as cheaply will be put out of business by competition. Surely, this is a 'most desirable' state of economic affairs. Or at least, that's what we are led to believe.

Let's take for example an Australian shoemaker who needs to sell a pair of shoes for $10 to remain economically viable. If an importer can import shoes of the same quality from Asia and sell them for $5, which pair of shoes are you going to buy?

Let us examine this situation a bit further: Where a local manufacturer may have to pay their workers $300 per week, the Asian manufacturer might only have to pay their workers $30 per month. So our local manufacturer has no hope of competing with their Asian counterpart and therefore, will go out of business. In the worst case scenario, they will end up on the dole with the government (i.e. you and me) supporting them and their family.

Further, if the importer knows that the cheapest pair of Australian-made shoes retail at $10 and they can profitably import the same shoes at $5, what will they charge for the imported shoes? No, silly, not $5. Why should they settle for that when they can safely charge $8 or $9.50 and still undercut the local product? So the pair of imported shoes was cheaper but you now have the financial cost of supporting an unemployed family and the social cost of that unemployment such as poverty, increased crime, etc. How cheap was that pair of shoes again?

If the cost of labour in all countries were identical, the open market approach would have some validity. But these costs are not and never have been identical, so why are we told the lie that a free market is to everyone's advantage? Asian workers work under sweat-shop conditions and are paid a pittance. Our workers are put out of jobs and will ultimately have to work for the same wages and under the same conditions as their Asian counterparts if they hope to compete in the jobs market. Again, we have international companies making money without any regard to the interests or needs of any individual or nation. And our governments are supporting this exploitation because those companies provide electoral funds for our politicians.

There are certain industries that a country should maintain as economically viable entities within its own boundaries. It should maintain its own food, clothing and shelter industries (I am not suggesting that this is actually done in Australia). If a country does not do this, it is left open to foreign economic blackmail and plunder. The present grinding down of our citrus industry is a sure-fire path to later economic disaster. It does not matter that our requirements can be imported more cheaply if a lack of them within the country leaves us vulnerable. Also, when industries remain within the country, the money we pay for their products also remains within the country and the country's wealth is not hived off to overseas interests.

Our politicians, having opened our markets to exploitative foreign competition then exhort us to 'buy Australian', knowing that we would have to be blockheads to do so (a pretty obvious hint as to what they really think of our intelligence). But it does sound patriotic, doesn't it?

Taxation

'The art of taxation is like the art of plucking geese - the aim is to extract the maximum number of feathers with the minimum amount of hissing.'

Jean-Baptiste Colbert (1619–1683)
French Treasurer

There are many enterprises (hospitals, roads, etc.), that need to be provided by the state. From this point of view, most of us accept the need for taxation. What many do not accept is the *extent* of taxation and the uses to which tax money is applied.

We are often told that the reason taxes are so high is because many citizens avoid paying their fair share and that the remainder of us are left to pay it. This is nonsense.

Governments will always levy enough tax to cover their spending needs. No person would pay any less tax even if there were no tax evasion — the government would simply call it a surplus and keep (or spend) it. Those who avoid tax at least ensure circulation of money within the economy so that it usually goes to more useful purposes than government enterprise.

There seems to be a level of taxation that people will accept without too much fuss. This level is about 10%. Most people realise that they are going to have this amount expropriated from them no matter what they do. Above this level, it is worth paying accountants and lawyers to find the loop holes to avoid it.

'If a rich merchant realises that he will be robbed every time he goes through Sherwood Forest, he soon learns not to go through Sherwood Forest.'

Laffer & Thomson

Those who avoid taxation are decried as bludging on the economy. On the other hand, the politicians who spend the proceeds quite liberally on themselves and their political parties are never criticised. It seems absurd that it should be antisocial not to contribute while it is okay to take whatever you want after the money has been put into the kitty.

It is also worth considering who actually pays the tax that is levied by the government. Tax is not necessarily paid by the person on whom it is levied. If, for example, the tax rate of doctors is increased, the doctor will simply increase his or her fees to cover that cost. So who is really paying the doctors' tax? The patient – *you.*

Not so long ago, State and Federal Governments decided to tax the banks on their turnover. This was called FID (Financial Institutions Duty) or BAD (Bank Accounts Debit tax). So what did the banks do? They simply charged it to the customers' accounts.

The present management of the US economy is certainly not looking to the future. With tax cuts, an increase in military expenditure and an increase in the budget deficit, the debts to be paid by future taxpayers are increasing exponentially. This may be good for the beneficiaries of the spending but it means disaster for the American economy.

Whenever people come to a situation where they find seemingly vast amounts available to spend, they spend it. Every survey of lottery winners shows that very few who won millions of dollars have much left over five years down the track. The same tendency applies to politicians. Where those who have minimal financial skills inherit a strong economy with a budget surplus, they very soon correct the imbalance.

If the effects of political mismanagement were immediately obvious, the perpetrators would be expelled from power before they could do too much damage. Unfortunately, there is a lag period. If an economy is expanding and the politicians do something to damage it, the economy will still continue to improve for a period of time before nose-diving. This is because the damage does not immediately affect work in progress. The reverse effect is also true — if the economy is going downhill and the politicians do something to improve it, there will also be a lag period in which the economy continues downwards for a short time before the results can be seen. This is popularly known as the 'J-Curve' effect.

An incoming government that inherits a budget surplus can claim the credit for it and one that inherits a deficit can blame the other side. People always see the economy as it presently is and are oblivious to what it was or might be.

PART IV

VIOLENCE AND WAR

16 TERRORISM AND VIOLENCE

Terrorism occurs when there is a threat of personal injury or death. It is simple, cheap and effective. Because it is simple, cheap and effective, terrorism can never be eradicated.

If you hold a gun to my head and demand my wallet, there is a good chance I will hand it over to you without further discussion. But what if you rang me up and said: 'I will be over at ten o'clock tonight for your wallet; please have it ready?' If you really want my wallet, which method do you think is going to be more effective?

There will always be schoolyard bullies; there will always be terrorism at all levels of society from the lowest to international levels. A 'war on terror' is a never-ending conflict. With such a perpetual phoney war, rulers can continue to infringe the rights of their own citizens forever.

Violence is a mechanism we all use to control our environment or to defend ourselves against it. The young child will kick and scream to get its own way. As we grow up, we find that violence does not always achieve the end we have in mind, so we work out more subtle and effective methods of achieving our objectives.

On September 11, 2001 (9/11), three aeroplanes deliberately crashed into the two towers of the New York's World Trade Center and the Pentagon. The explanation given to the public was that Muslim fanatics 'hate our way of life' and seek to wipe us out. Really? Are these people so fanatical that they are prepared to sacrifice their lives simply because they don't like us? To anyone looking at western intervention in the Middle East, it is a no-brainer to understand why the bombing happened in 2001.

Since the end of the Second World War, there has scarcely been a year that the US military has not bombed some foreign country. For a decade prior to the final invasion of Iraq, the US had repeatedly been bombing large areas of Iraq under the pretence that they were protecting the civilian population. Nobody seems to appreciate that the bombing was actually killing civilians.

The Arab nationalists were saying to the American people: 'Your government has been bombing us for years. This is what it is like to be bombed, Yanks, how do you like it?' Like so many violent acts that are meant to get a message across, the message often gets lost in translation. If someone sinks a boot into your posterior, your first response will be more likely to return the favour than to enter into an intellectual debate. It does not matter that the boot in the posterior was to urge you to be more respectful to your elders and betters; you are more likely to be affronted than thankful.

A violent act initiated as a lesson to someone else often becomes a tit-for-tat reaction.

Scenario A:

1. Muslims bomb the World Trade Center in New York to give Americans a lesson in what it is like to be bombed.

2. Trade Center bombing causes retaliation by invading Afghanistan.

3. Invasion of Afghanistan causes retaliation by Bali bombers causing the deaths of 200 foreigners (including 88 Australians).

4. Deaths of 88 Australians results in calls for deaths of bombers...etc.

Scenario B:

1. IRA activists bomb Protestants to deter them from molesting IRA supporters in Northern Ireland.

2. Protestants retaliate by bombing IRA targets.

3. IRA activists retaliate by bombing Protestants.

4. Protestants retaliate by...etc.

Similarly, the Trade Center bombings looked more like the initiation of a war than a polite request to stop bombing Muslims. For that reason, the US administration was able to use it as an excuse to bomb Afghanistan. I must admit that the logic of laying waste to a whole country in order to catch a single terrorist escapes me.

Some 750,000 civilians have already died in Iraq as a result of the US military intervention. The US has thus killed more than *two hundred times* the number of people killed in the World Trade Center bombings, and Iraq had *nothing* to do with the bombings in New York.

We, in the west, do not see the bloodshed and heartache of the western war on the Muslim citizens of the Middle East — that would not look nice in our newspapers. We never see our bombs hitting civilian targets. We rarely see any evidence that Iraqi human beings have been hurt. All we see is the precision bombing of 'terrorist' targets and the swift removal of 'insurgents' with missiles guided from aircraft. It might be noted that our missiles only kill insurgents and terrorists—never civilians—and that is why they are called 'smart bombs'! We rarely see the tears in the eyes of the Iraqis whose families have been destroyed and who are asking the same questions that New Yorkers asked after they were bombed: 'What have we done to deserve this?'

A term 'war on terror', is nonsense because 'terror' is a state of mind. It has no substance. One cannot shoot down ideas with bullets. The reason we fall for this government propaganda is because we equate 'war on terror' with 'guarantee of safety'. Regardless of the fear generated by such propaganda, the fact is that you have a greater chance of being struck by lightning than of being hurt by a terrorist. If we are struck with fear and convinced that terrorists are lurking behind every lamp post and under every bed, we will accept that the government may take whatever steps are necessary to guard us – no matter how ridiculous or extreme those steps really are.

We are told that these terrorists need to be put in detention beyond the reach of civilian laws. Civilian laws and principles have been developed over centuries to ensure justice and provide protection for the citizen against the tyranny of the state. What state secret is protected by not allowing lawyers and relatives access to a prisoner? And what valuable information will one get from a person who has been in detention for five or six years? The only reason to keep something secret is if you do not want anyone else to know about it. Now, why would the authorities not want us to know how they are interrogating prisoners?

There can be only one purpose in indefinite detention

without charge or legal representation, and that is to permit torture and coerce confessions.

We were told that a 'terrorist' is presumed to be innocent until proven guilty. This is clearly absurd. To be gaoled indefinitely without charge is surely a presumption of guilt. If you look at the latest counter-terrorism laws in Australia, you will note that they deny even the basic rights of established law. As things stand, any politician can simply designate an opponent as a terrorist and have him or her gaoled. The victim will have no right to reclaim their freedom and no access to legal representation. And if someone has information that a person has been arrested, that person is breaking the law if he or she tells anyone else that this has occurred. The result is that the authorities can arrest anyone, conceal their place of confinement and, indeed, even murder them without anyone knowing. And if anyone tells, they are likely to suffer the same fate.

With all of this evidence, can anyone possibly believe that the so-called 'anti-terror' laws are really enacted to protect us from terrorists? You will note that it is politicians and state authorities who decide who shall be designated a terrorist, not a court or independent tribunal. The laws are designed to incarcerate any person the politician wishes to incarcerate and to deny that person rights that even our worst criminals are granted. Anti-terror laws are designed to protect politicians from citizens — not to protect citizens from terrorists.

'It is a general popular error to suppose the loudest complainants for the public to be the most anxious for its welfare.'
Edmund Burke (1729–1797)

Causes of Middle Eastern Terrorism

From the way our politicians talk, one would think that certain Muslim fanatics have simply decided, on a religious basis, that they do not like western ideals and will therefore wage war on westerners. Now why would anybody sacrifice his or her own life to kill someone simply because they despised the way that person chose to live?

The unknown always presents fears. And it is easy for politicians to generate fear of Muslims because they are foreigners, wear different clothes and believe in an alien religion. Anyone with those characteristics must be evil. We were led to believe that Muslims worship some strange God, even though 'Allah' is Arabic for 'God' and it is exactly the same God worshipped by Jews and Christians.

Our media always use a term 'Muslim fanatics' and not 'Arab fanatics', because that might alienate the affections of Saudi Arabia (even though the bombers of the World Trade Center were all Saudis). We never seem to hear of Catholic or Protestant 'fanatics' fighting in Northern Ireland. Our politicians are always quick to cover their fear-mongering by saying that not all Muslims are bad, it is only that the minority of them are fanatics. They are trying to have two bob each way — they want to create a general fear of Muslims in the minds of westerners but they also want Muslims to believe that their rhetoric is not anti-Islam.

The US and Britain have invaded both Afghanistan and Iraq without legitimate cause with the resultant deaths of hundreds of thousands of innocent civilians. Even the first Gulf War of 1990–91 against Iraq had dubious legitimacy. The economic sanctions on Iraq that followed this war had little effect on the Iraqi leadership, but led to further deaths and suffering of thousands of Iraqi civilians. It was estimated that some 500,000 Iraqi children died as a result of these sanctions in the decade that followed the first Gulf War. What is also not widely recognised is the fact that the US supplied Saddam Hussein with the chemical and biological weapons he used against his own people.

Armed with the above facts and knowing that Iraq has enormous oil reserves, what credence can any rational person put on the American claim that they invaded Iraq to bring democracy and freedom to the people? America's love of democracy never extends to despotic regimes that support the US; its desire to spread democracy seems confined to states that presently oppose it. The US politicians used to tell us that they could not leave Iraq 'until the job was done'. Well, they did leave Iraq without doing anything of significance except destroying the country.

It is very strange how the Arab mind cannot comprehend that Britain, the US and Australia are really the champions of goodness and niceness, and that their homes and children are being destroyed only *for their own good!*

Prior to the invasion of Afghanistan and Iraq, Middle Eastern countries had no reason to want revenge against Australia. To believe that our part in that invasion has made us safer from terrorism is just plain poppycock. No Australian citizens were endangered prior to the invasion of Afghanistan. Since then we have had the Bali bombings, which cost us 88 Australian lives. This blood is squarely on the hands of the Australian government. All of our anti-terrorism laws have been introduced purely as a result of the danger the Australian government has, itself, created. We now have security processes at all airports that are costing the Australian taxpayer millions of dollars and which provide no greater security than we previously had. We are constantly told that the security measures are working because we have had no terrorist threats since their introduction. The security measures must have a retrospective effect because they prevented terrorist threats *before* their introduction also!

This reminds me of the old story about the neighbour who was dusting his front fence with a white powder:

'Why are you doing that?' he was asked.
'To keep the tigers away', he replied.
'But there aren't any tigers here.'
'Effective, isn't it?'

We are now starting to learn the truth of torture and abuses of human rights at the Abu Ghraib and Guantanamo Bay prisons. To suggest these abuses were due to a small minority of 'bad apples' is really the same as asking us to believe that pigs might fly. Of course, the terrorism comes from higher up the chain of command.

The Geneva Conventions and the international agreements against torture have been blatantly ignored by the American and Australian administrations. The Geneva Conventions and latterly, the Treaty of Rome state quite explicitly that the conventions cannot be over-ridden by a country simply declaring them to be inapplicable. The Treaty of Rome has been signed by both the US and Australia, but not ratified by the US (so much for the integrity of the Australian government in honouring its international treaty obligations). If we unilaterally ignore the Geneva Conventions today, what is to stop our enemy ignoring them tomorrow?

The following statements come from US Supreme Court Judge, Robert Jackson, the chief US prosecutor at the Nuremberg trials:

An aggressor is the first to commit such actions as invasion of its armed forces, with or without a declaration of war, of the territory of another state.'

Where does this definition place Australia and

the US in relation to the invasion of Iraq?

'If certain acts of violations of treaties are crimes, they are crimes whether the US does them or whether Germany does them and we are not prepared to lay down a rule of criminal conduct against others which we would not be willing to have invoked against us.'

What, then, is the status of the bombing of Dresden, the fire-bombing of Tokyo and the atom bombings of Hiroshima and Nagasaki in relation to this statement?

'We must never forget that the record on which we judge these defendants is the record on which history will judge us tomorrow. To pass these defendants a poisoned chalice is to put it to our own lips as well.'

Are we prepared to sip from the poisoned chalice of torture and abuse that we have passed to those we have attacked in the Middle East?

Thank God for short memories.

17 WAR

'Man's inhumanity to man makes countless thousands mourn.'

Robert Burns (1759–1796)

During the First World War, the US supplied Britain with arms. The expense of the First World War effectively cost Britain its empire, but America became economically stronger by selling arms and keeping out of conflicts. At the time America became involved in 1917, the war was virtually over; whichever side America decided to favour would be the winning side.

In the Second World War , the US also entered late, again to the benefit of its economy. Some unkind observers have been heard to say that the only reason the US entered the Second World War was because they were 'Pearl-Harboured' into it.

The obvious lesson is to keep out of war but provide arms to the belligerents. When a country is involved in wars, the cost of buying the arms, even from the country's own industrialists, is a certain way to wipe out its economy. It may be that history will validate the

American approach, but like the Scotsman, 'A have ma doots'.

It is often said that nobody wants wars. Regrettably, this is not a quite true. If nobody wanted wars, there would be no wars. Virtually every war is fought for profit or commercial advantage. After the attack on Iraq, the first areas secured by the US army were the oilfields. The excuse that Iraq was invaded to protect its citizens and bring democracy seems rather hollow when one sees the other oppressed nations in the Middle East and Africa where dictatorships are supported by the US.

There is a thriving background industry which is pocketing billions of taxpayers' dollars. This is the armaments business. The prices of arms and munitions are well over and above the real cost. Guided missiles cost millions of dollars and can only be used once. Has anyone ever provided a real costing of these? Does the real cost of materials and labour for a missile really amount to millions of dollars? Munitions manufacturing is therefore a very profitable business, so you can understand the motives of these people.

Politicians are in constant need of money and what better place to get it than from those who have some to spare. The large and profitable industrial complexes provide election funds to the politicians and in return, the politicians make the laws and determine budget outlays. There is thus a symbiotic relationship between the ruling politicians and the rulers of industry. The politicians divert funds to big business and big business diverts some of this back to political campaigns. These funds originate with the taxpayer who also provides the gun-fodder for war. This is a real double whammy! You not only pay for the war, but you also get to be part it. Wars are never fought by the politicians or businessmen who start them, but by the average citizens who believe they are fighting for a better world.

If all the US armed forces were disbanded tomorrow, the country would go into a severe economic depression because of the number of people in the military and those dependent on it. America cannot afford to abolish its military.

The politicians, however, face a problem. How do you convince a nation that it needs a large army if there is no danger? No problem. Simply create a danger and maintain the illusion that the country is under constant threat of attack. The people need to be kept in fear. In the past, there was the threat of the Soviet Union, which was, at least, capable of a credible attack. Nowadays we have no obvious hostile country that could take on the might of the US. The dangers of such countries as Afghanistan and Iraq are invented. How either of these countries could pose a threat to the US or us is beyond the scope of an average person's imagination.

Our rulers even go further—they are now fighting a *war on terror!* This is totally absurd. 'Terror' is a concept; it has no concrete substance. You cannot shoot down an idea with bullets. How can any military force ever win a war on terrorism? The answer is that it can't, and, what is more, it never intended to. The talk of a war on terrorism is to fuel fear in the populace and justify military spending. Terrorism is an eternal excuse. The attacks on Iraq had nothing to do with terrorism — it was all to do with political control. The fact that thousands of innocent civilians die as a result of these onslaughts is of a little concern to the politicians — control and oil profits take precedence. Nor do the governments take any responsibility for the thousands of their own soldiers who are sacrificed needlessly. A tear in the eye and the solemn placing of a wreath are all that is needed to pacify the ignorant masses.

Our governments are far from the benevolent institutions we might believe or want them to be.

Governments of the 20th century have repeatedly shown themselves to be traitors to their own people and to humanity as a whole. As we shall see, the rise of Hitler and the carnage of the World War II were supported and encouraged by western governments. Hitler could have never risen to power without the tacit approval of the British and French governments. The leaders knew they were betraying their people at the time. When Daladier, the French Prime Minister, returned to Paris after the Munich meeting, which signed Czechoslovakia over to Hitler, he expected vilification from the French crowds. To his amazement, he was given a hero's welcome. At this, he was heard to say *'Les cons'*, broadly translated meaning of 'the bloody idiots'. Even today our governments are betraying us without the slightest ethical qualms. How can one possibly justify the bombing and destruction of Afghanistan on the basis that it harbours terrorists? You don't need an entire country to train soldiers or terrorists.

Would one destroy Sydney on suspicions that a mafia gang had a safe-house there? And why would one bomb Afghanistan when the terrorists were Saudi nationals?

War is only an extension of national diplomacy. If diplomacy fails, then war is the next step. Wars increase a nation's power or economic advantage; they are never initiated for ethical reasons or to provide a good for anyone but the aggressor.

There are two classic treatises on war:

The Art of War, Sun Tzu (Chinese military treatise, 6th century BCE)
The Principles of War, Carl von Clausewitz (1780–1831)

Most observers agree that the Vietnam War would never have been waged by the US if the generals had only read the book by Sun Tzu. (Nobody who could read any book would have started the war in Iraq.)

18 | WORLD WAR II

Many people have called Hitler a madman who brought carnage to Europe. Carnage certainly occurred, but was Hitler really mad? I have often wondered how one man could come from obscurity to gain control of virtually all of continental Europe in the space of twenty years. It seems rather trite to simply dismiss him as a madman. Whether he was mad or not, how did he do it? The answer, unfortunately, is not very pretty.

In 1918, Germany could see that it was not going to win World War I. An Armistice was signed and the guns fell silent on November 11th of that year. This was to be followed by another meeting which the Germans thought was going to be a conference to thrash out the terms of surrender. When the unconditional surrender treaty was presented at Versailles, some of the German generals, who regarded this as a betrayal of the Armistice agreement, refused to sign. Ultimately, the Treaty of Versailles was signed as the Germans realised they were in no position to restart the war. The reparations imposed on Germany were exceedingly heavy and virtually every commentator has agreed that they were grossly unfair.

As a result of the burden of the treaty and the subsequent humiliation of the German people, Hitler was able to generate support for his Nazi party. This party did create employment and restored the sense of pride in the German people. Hitler increased employment by developing a military capacity. He began to build battleships, submarines and tanks and increased the numbers of military personnel. He sent forces to occupy the Rhineland, the western part of Germany abutting France. On being ordered into the Rhineland, the German generals almost had a seizure as they felt sure the French would blow them to kingdom come. Britain and France did nothing and did not even suggest to Hitler that he might have made a mistake. After receiving no opposition, Hitler sent forces into Austria and absorbed it into the Reich. This was also contrary to the Treaty of Versailles, but again, Britain and France did nothing. Hitler decided next that he wanted Czechoslovakia, particularly the Sudetenland – the area with a majority German population. Czechoslovakia was created as an independent state at the end of the First World War and its integrity was guaranteed under treaty by France, Britain and the Soviet Union (the Soviet Union, however, only guaranteed to defend it providing France sent troops first). So when Hitler asked for the Sudetenland, Chamberlain and Daladier, the British and French Prime Ministers, met Hitler in Munich and agreed to cede the abovementioned territory in exchange for 'peace in our time' as Chamberlain later described it. They did not bother to include the Czechoslovakian Prime Minister, Benes, or the Soviet Union in these talks.

Let us stop at this stage to inject a bit of logic into the argument:

Germany had lost the First World War and, under the terms of the Treaty of Versailles, was not permitted to expand its armed forces or materiel, and was not to occupy the Rhineland. When Hitler started building battleships and submarines, what did Britain and France think was going on? Did they think that this was simply some cool method for reducing unemployment? Can anyone really believe that the British and French governments had no idea that such armaments might be used for warlike purposes? Or did they think Hitler was going to trade them for sea-shells with South Sea natives? When there were huge torchlight parades of thousands of military-looking personnel in Germany did they think this was some extravagant boy-scout jamboree?

And what about Czechoslovakia? Britain and France *had* guaranteed to protect its integrity. Why didn't they honour their agreement? At the time, the Sudetenland of Czechoslovakia had very strong fortifications in mountainous country. The Czechs also had one of the most powerful armies in Europe with eighteen active army divisions (an army division consists of about 16,000–20,000 personnel). At the same time, Germany had less than forty available divisions. If Hitler had to take Czechoslovakia by military force, he would have had a tough battle on his hands. The famous *Blitzkrieg* (lightning war) that he later used against Poland would also have been virtually useless because of the geography of Czechoslovakia.

So, why didn't Britain and France stop Hitler at the early stages when it would be dead easy? It is nonsense to say they appeased Hitler to prevent a war. All they had to do was to say no when Hitler first started to violate the Treaty of Versailles and before he could build up a significant military capacity. Indeed, Hitler admitted that the entrance of German forces into the Rhineland were the most worrying 48 hours of his life.

The answer to the above question again lies in events towards the end of the World War I:

In October 1917, the Russian Revolution began.

This led to the overthrow of the Tsar and the usurpation of government by the Mensheviks. The Mensheviks were reasonably moderate but were soon displaced by the hard left-wingers, the Bolsheviks, who established a Socialist government. This took Russia out of the First World War. As the Russian Socialist government flag was red, they became known as the Reds and its army became known as the Red Army. There were, of course, counter-insurgents to the Red Army takeover. These were known as the White Russians.

The western powers (Britain, France and the USA) had large financial interests in Russia at the time. Thus, they were less than amused by the state of play in Russia and certainly did not want anyone to get the impression that the hoi-polloi should be allowed to run any country. They therefore lent support to the White Russians in the hope that they would regain power for the proper ruling class. In April 1920, Poland invaded Russia with the backing of Britain and France. Lloyd-George, the British Prime Minister at the time, ordered a shipload of arms to be sent to Poland to support this invasion. However, the British dock-workers refused to load the ship, which happened to be aptly named 'The Jolly George'. In August 1920, the Red Army drove the Polish invading forces back to its own borders. Lloyd-George now threatened to send troops to aid the Poles. However, the British Labour Party and the Trade Unions organised a 'Council of Action', which had the power to call a general strike if British forces attacked Russia. This presented Lloyd-George with a problem. The term 'Soviet' is Russian for 'council' or 'worker's council'. The trade union 'Council of Action' was starting to look dangerously like the advent of Socialism into Britain itself. Lloyd-George obviously came to the rapid conclusion that further provocation might be unwise.

Also during 1920, the French fleet mutinied in the Black Sea to stop French intervention against the

Bolsheviks. Mutiny is not something a military person undertakes lightly so the French government presumably came to the same conclusions as Lloyd-George.

Hitler had always maintained that the German people needed more living space (Lebensraum) and had made no secret that he felt the best open space lay to the east. What more could a British and French government ask for than a conquered nation being prepared to risk the lives of its people to get rid of an unwanted Russian government? And at no cost to the British or French either. Hitler was the answer to a maiden's prayer.

A part of German Prussia had been ceded to Poland at the end of the World War I. The Poles acquired the German port of Danzig (present day, Gdansk) and hence access to the Baltic Sea. Hitler felt that this should be returned to the Reich.

The British would probably have had no particular objection to the above, if they did not have to face two problems:

1. They had a treaty with Poland to come to its aid if it encountered aggression. As we shall see, honouring treaty obligations has never been a high priority for Britain and this problem could have been simply overcome had it not been for the second problem.

2. The British public was becoming restive about Hitler's territorial conquests and were looking to their government to do something about it.

Winston Churchill was also rocking the boat by criticising Prime Minister Chamberlain's actions in respect to Czechoslovakia. (It seems as though nobody had bothered to tell Churchill what the game plan was.) If Hitler had only known who his real friends were and had exerted a little restraint, he could probably take Poland without a fight as well. He could then have taken as much Russian *lebensraum* as he liked. But we are straying into alternate universes.

Hitler wanted to take a hunk of Poland but he knew that Britain and France had treaty obligations and the war with them would be unavoidable. He certainly did not want Russia entering the fray and thereby muddying the waters. Therefore, he was busting to seal a non-aggression pact with the Soviet Union.

Stalin, however, could see Germany's territorial ambitions and wanted to sign a mutual co-operation pact with Britain and France. He put this proposition to Chamberlain and Daladier and asked for their support to convince the Polish government to allow Soviet troops to advance over Polish territory. The Poles, understandably, were less than delighted with this proposition as they had been lucky to return with their pants on after attacking Russia less than 20 years previously.

The British and French kept stalling with respect to any treaty agreement. When Stalin asked Chamberlain how many troops Britain would send if they went to war with Germany, Chamberlain replied: *'Two Divisions now and two Divisions later.'* Stalin responded: *'If Russia has to go to war, I estimate I will need to put up 300 Divisions.'* Stalin got the message. The Soviet–German non-aggression pact was signed soon thereafter.

Even when Hitler attacked Poland, Britain and France sat on their hands for as long as they could. German general Alfred Jodl stated at the Nuremberg trials: *'If we did not collapse already in the year 1939 that was due only to the fact that during the Polish campaign, the approximately 110 French and British divisions in the West were completely inactive against the 23 German divisions.'*

What? Britain and France were at war with Germany, had a military superiority of almost 5:1 and didn't fire a shot? Loose lips sink ships, Herr Jodl. To the gallows with you!

Another peculiar and little known episode of the Second World War also deserves mention. On June 27, 1942, Convoy PQ17, escorted by ten British warships and four support cruisers, left Reykjavik, Iceland, for Archangel, Russia. On July 4, the support cruisers were ordered to withdraw (taking with them six out of the ten escort vessels), and the convoy was ordered to 'scatter'. The reason given for this order was that the British Admiralty feared attack by German naval vessels. The convoy thus became a sitting duck for the German Luftwaffe. Only eleven of the original thirty-six ships made it to Archangel.

There are a number of points about this episode that arouse suspicion:

1. Why was the convoy escorted by warships if an attack by German vessels was not expected in the first place?

2. Why did this episode occur almost immediately after a meeting between Russian Foreign Minister Molotov and US President Roosevelt?

In May 1942, Molotov went to the US to beg for an opening of a second front against Germany in order to prevent annihilation of the Red Army. Even though his generals told him that the opening of this front was impossible at this time, Roosevelt promised that a second front would be opened later in 1942. No front was opened in 1942 and no serious attempt was made to open one until June 6, 1944 (D-Day). Indeed, the D-Day landings only took place after it looked like the Soviet Union was going to defeat Germany.

1. Contrary to the advice of all but one of his staff, Lord Pound (First Sea Lord from 1939 to 1943) ordered dispersal of the convoy. This aberration by Lord

Pound was later excused on the basis that he had a brain tumour. (I, for one, would want to see the pathological specimen of Lord Pound's brain before I would swallow this one!).

2. The convoy carried enough aeroplanes, tanks and trucks to equip an army of 50,000.

3. The sinking of this convoy was used as an excuse to delay the sending of the next convoy (PQ18).

By a strange coincidence, the Battle for Stalingrad, one of the bloodiest battles of World War II, began two weeks later.

It seems hard to escape the conclusion that the British vessels and their crews were deliberately sacrificed in order to deny supply to Russia and basically to wipe out the Red Army. This incident was far too outrageous to be regarded as just a normal British Naval cock-up.

If the aim of Britain and France was to damage the Soviet Union, they certainly made a good fist of it. Some twenty million Russians died as a result of the Second World War and Soviet soldiers' deaths made about half of that number.

Allied European Military Casualties of World War II:

	Number	(%)
Soviet Union	10,700,000	91.31
USA	416,800	3.56
Great Britain	382,700	3.27
France	217,600	1.86
TOTAL	**11,717,100**	**100.00**

Gee, I always thought America won World War II!

When we look back on the circumstances, we cannot avoid the conclusion that the western powers encouraged Germany to build up forces to do what they had been unable to do — attack and (hopefully) destroy the Soviet Union. If you had been the British Prime Minister at the time and saw your enemy of yesterday building up forces against its treaty obligations, what would you have done? Also consider how many of your own people had been killed in the First World War. Would you have allowed Germany to get into a position to counter-attack and repeat the carnage of the last effort?

Is it surprising that the Soviet Union maintained suppression of Germany for decades after the end of the Second World War? Is it surprising that the Russia today does not trust the build-up of US 'star wars' facilities on its borders? An explanation that the US anti-missile defence in Poland are construed as a defence against Iranian missiles and not as a threat to Russia requires us to leave our brains at home. Are we to believe that the Iranians will send missiles up along the western border of Russia where they will then do a sharp left hand turn to the west through Poland?

But then we have been invited to believe similar absurdities in the past: witness the magic bullet that killed President Kennedy. This also did three or four unexplained sharp turns during its travels, and people believed that! Present US President Obama has recently cancelled the anti-missile defence in Poland. Opponents to this change have pointed out that this will encourage Russia to become more belligerent. So much for the original claim that the Polish missile project had nothing to do with Russia!

The carnage of World War II may have been a result of Germany's accession to power, but that attainment could have never occurred without the British and French governments selling out their own people.

It is obvious that our politicians march to the beat of a different drum than that of the common citizen. We have more than adequate evidence that our politicians repeatedly lie to us. We have incontrovertible evidence they are prepared to dishonour any agreements they make without compunction. We have evidence they will sell out their armed forces and sacrifice their own people whenever it suits them. But, in fairness, they are 'men of principle'; they will always defend their principles to the last drop of anyone else's blood.

'History is but a fable that has been agreed upon.'
Napoleon Bonaparte (1769–1821)

'The history of wars is always written by the victors.'
Winston Churchill (1874–1965)

19 WAR CRIMES TRIBUNALS

After World War II, the Nuremberg trials were instituted to try the perpetrators of Nazi war crimes. On the surface, this sounds admirable and no one suggests that criminals should not be brought to justice. But is justice the prime motivating factor? I do not recall War Crimes Tribunals following any previous wars. Why this one?

There are too many episodes related to the Second World War that cast suspicion on the French, British and US governments. If the top Nazi operatives could openly tell all they knew of the secret agreements between Germany and western governments, perhaps the picture might not be so convenient. The statement by German general Jodl mentioned earlier was certainly not flattering to the victors. What would be the consequences if the alleged criminals told the Soviet Union what agreements had been made between the high commands of Germany and the western allies?

Most of the captured senior Nazis were ultimately executed except for two: Hermann Goering who 'committed suicide' in his cell a day before his hanging, and Rudolf Hess, imprisoned in Spandau prison for the remainder of his life. During this time neither he nor his visitors were permitted to discuss anything to do with the war. Dead men tell no tales!

If we turn to the war in Iraq, we see the same pattern again. All of the senior members of the Saddam regime were executed for war crimes. 'Chemical Ali' was executed for using poison gas on the Kurds. This gas was supplied by the US. What did the US administrators think it was going to be used for? Perhaps for an exotic new perfume for Saddam's harem?

By all means, war criminals must be brought to justice. But, having convicted them, we should allow journalists free access to hear their side of the story and test their assertions. (Saddam Hussein did offer to debate US President George Bush about the Iraq war but his offer was not taken up. I wonder why?) We might find more war criminals than we expected. Of course I jest. If we executed all war criminals, who would be left to run our countries?

Having given Germany a guilt trip about the Second World War, perhaps, in fairness, we should list some allied war crimes of World War II. These were cases of deliberate attacks on unarmed civilians in which there was no valid military objective:

1.   The bombing of Dresden
2.   The fire-bombing of Tokyo
3.   The atomic bombing of Hiroshima and Nagasaki

There are three good reasons why the atomic bomb should never have been dropped on the innocent civilians of Hiroshima and Nagasaki:

1. Most of the scientists who developed the bomb never anticipated it would be used against civilians and had suggested that a demonstration device be dropped off the coast of Japan in some safe location.

(The chief scientist, Oppenheimer, apparently had no objections.)

2. President Truman had intelligence that the Japanese war effort was finished and the Japanese were only waiting for a face-saving way of surrendering.

3. General Dwight Eisenhower had told Truman that such an act was unnecessary.

In spite of these reasons, Truman ordered bombs to be dropped, not only on civilians but at a time when he knew children would be on their way to school. His rationale was that the destruction of children would make the Japanese High Command agree to an immediate unconditional surrender. He was right.

If, during a war, one may take any action which might shorten that war, then there is no such thing as a war crime.

Winners of wars never face trial for any crimes they commit. Thus, war crimes will never be stopped because everyone fighting a war expects to win.

"The belief that Might makes Right is clearly stated to be the basis of the trials the United States has conducted at Nuremberg. 'We sit,' said the American judges, 'as a Tribunal drawing its sole power and jurisdiction from the will and command of the four occupying powers... In so far as Control Council Law No.10 may be thought to go beyond established principles of international law, its authority, of course, rests upon the exercise of the 'sovereign legislative power' of the countries to which the German Reich unconditionally surrendered.

Few Americans at home may be aware of it, but their representatives at Nuremberg have expressly stated that the victors are not bound by the same laws as the vanquished. When the German defence counsel argued that if it was a crime against international law for the Germans in occupied Poland and Russia to confiscate private property, use civilians and prisoners of war as forced labourers, and starve the people in the occupied territories, then why is it not also a crime for American, British, French or Russian Military Government to do the same thing, they were told:

'The Allied Powers are not subject to the limitations of the Hague Convention and rules of land warfare.'

'Why?'

'Because,' said the American judges and prosecutors at Nuremberg, 'the rules of land warfare apply to the conduct of a belligerent in occupied territory so long as there is an army in the field attempting to restore the country to its true owner, but these rules do not apply when belligerency is ended, there is no longer any army in the field, and, as in the case of Germany, subjugation has occurred by virtue of military conquest.'

In other words, if Germany had won the war, it would have ceased to be bound by international law, and none of its nationals could be held guilty of having committed war crimes or 'crimes against humanity.' Since we won it, we are not limited in any way by provisions of Hague or Geneva Conventions, or by any international or recognised law."

This theory was given immediate application after Germany's surrender. Many German prisoners of war in American hands, who had hitherto been decently treated, suddenly found themselves transformed into men of no rights, liable to be forced to work long hours for a pittance in consequence of a disposition made in Washington. Instead of being sent home at the war's end, according to the Geneva Convention, their American captors handed them over to the French to be used as slave labourers in mines and factories. The French thereupon deprived them even of their warm clothing and the dollars they had earned as prisoners of war. The British similarly kept German prisoners of war as forced labourers for years after the end of the war."

The High Cost of Vengeance Freda Utley (1949 Henry Regnery Company) Extract from Chapter 6

It is perfectly clear that the Nuremberg War Crimes Tribunals didn't even pretend to be courts of justice, but this is how it must be if you want to be sure of exterminating *all* of the witnesses against you.

20 | IRAQ AND AFGHANISTAN

Why was Afghanistan invaded by coalition forces? We were originally told that the purpose of the invasion was to capture Osama Bin Laden. But after seven years of war, this capture never eventuated. Now we are told that our purpose in Afghanistan is to defeat the Taliban. This was never the original purpose. The Taliban were originally told that if they did not surrender Osama Bin Laden, then they would be invaded. Why is the Taliban now the enemy? Laying waste to a whole country is a rather circuitous way of finding one man, and is the benefit proportional to the cost?

We must stay in Afghanistan, of course, because this is a war we cannot afford to lose. But, what if we do lose? When you want to win a war, you have less than a 50% chance of doing so. And how will we know if we have won? No politician will define the final objective of the war. As soon as one objective is reached another one is found. The reality is that we will continue to be involved in war until adequate profits have been made or until the populace rebels against it. Crocodile tears over the graves of sacrificed soldiers are only effective for a limited time.

For those who have lost loved ones as a result of these wars, take comfort in the belief that your son lost his life for a worthy cause even though no-one will ever be able to tell you what that cause was.

The predictive powers of our politicians are nothing short of mind-blowing. These are the people who could not see a global financial catastrophe one month in advance, but they can accurately predict what will happen in ten years if we don't fight in Afghanistan. There is the possibility that we may achieve nothing in Afghanistan. What then? Should we all buy pistols to commit suicide when the Taliban take over? We were also told that we had to fight in Korea to save the world. We did not win that one and the world did not change. We were also told that we had to fight in Vietnam to save the world. We actually lost that one and again, the world did not change. We were also told that we had to fight in Iraq to save the world and we achieved nothing there. We are all still here and we have never yet had to submit to the evil hordes from the North. Of course, the result could be quite different if they knew where Australia was.

The invasion of Iraq was clearly illegal under International Law as there never was any UN resolution that directed that Iraq should be invaded. The original purpose of the Iraq invasion was to remove 'weapons of mass destruction'. No such weapons were ever found, but allied forces remained with the following consecutive set of excuses:

1. To remove Saddam Hussein.
2. To bring security to the country.
3. To stay until 'the job is done' – whatever that mythical job was.

Now, with no evidence that security had improved one jot or tittle, our forces have been removed.

There is no provision under International Law for a 'pre-emptive' strike on another nation. In fact, such a strike was clearly defined as 'aggression' by the American prosecutor at the Nuremberg trials following World War II. There is provision for a first strike when there is a clear and imminent threat of danger, but the invasion of Iraq came nowhere near this definition.

During the Afghan conflict, many prisoners were taken, mostly by the local militias. In order to gather intelligence information, the US army paid these militias to bring prisoners in.

The US must have the only army in the world that has ever had to buy prisoners.

Even the treatment of the prisoners has no logical or legal justification. If the war in Afghanistan is a '*war* on terrorism', why are prisoners not being treated as prisoners of war? To abduct them from Afghanistan and imprison them in wire cages on the beaches of Cuba is contrary to all of the accepted rules of war. And after five years' incarceration, how could they possibly give any information of value? And if they were guilty of any crimes, how come no convincing evidence of it can be found after five years? Not only can't we win wars, we can't even lose them charitably. The danger of this behaviour is that other nations now have no moral obligation to comply with the international conventions either.

Even if the imagination is stretched to its limits, the invasion of Iraq had no relevance to the national interests of Australia. Why, then, was Australia involved in the invasion? Military people enlist in order to defend their country. It is surely treason against our soldiers to risk their lives in an adventure that has no relevance to the defence of this country. Why are Australian soldiers being risked to fight in someone else's war?

Not only the lives of our soldiers are being risked, but the danger to every Australian has been massively increased as a result of our intervention in Afghanistan. We have already lost 88 Australian lives in the Bali bombings and the bill for increased security measures now amounts to millions of dollars per year – all because of an invasion that had no validity in the first place. How much more is our government's stupidity going to cost us in the future?

The same government that sent our soldiers to fight for the freedom of Afghans and Iraqis has the impertinence to say to the world: 'We will determine who enters our country and the terms under which they come.' Why weren't Iraq and Afghanistan afforded this privilege too? I am so glad I that I belong to a master race and not to some inferior one.

It was estimated by a Nobel laureate in economics that if one-sixth of the money spent on the Iraq war by the US had been earmarked for the provision of health care to children in the US, then their health would be guaranteed for the next fifty years. President Bush vetoed any increase in health care funding for US children. There are such things as priorities!

21 | ARAB–ISRAELI CONFLICT

If we look to the Middle East and observe the wars and tensions between Israel and the surrounding Arab nations, we tend to be puzzled. Why won't those terrible Arabs simply leave Israel alone? The Jews are surely entitled to a safe homeland after all of the persecutions they have suffered throughout history, not the least being the holocaust inflicted by the Nazis during World War II. In order to understand the situation, there are some facts we first need to know.

Towards the end of the 19th century, there was growing pressure within the Jewish community to establish a Jewish homeland (the Zionist movement). In the beginning of the 20th century, small Jewish communities started to set up communes (Kibbutzim) in Palestine.

Prior to World War I, Palestine had been a part of the Ottoman (Turkish) Empire. In order to defeat the Turks, the British sent Lieutenant-Colonel T.E. Lawrence, alias Lawrence of Arabia, to organise Arab resistance to the Turkish forces. Lawrence was told to promise post-war autonomy to the Arabs as a reward for their support, which he did. Towards the end of the war, it became clear that Britain had no intention of honouring this promise. Lawrence was devastated because it was his word that the Arabs trusted. (And some people wonder why Britain is known as 'Perfidious Albion'!)

During World War I, the British were interested in using cordite as a fuse for explosives. The trade secret for this was owned by Chaim Weizmann (1874–1952), a Jewish Zionist. When asked what he wanted in return for permission to use cordite, Weizmann replied: 'A homeland for my people.' This was an understandable request considering the number of organised persecutions of Jews over the centuries. These ranged from the imposition of anti-Jewish laws to confinement to special areas (ghettos) to outright murder.

In 1917, a secret note was sent from the British government to Weizmann, which became known as the Balfour Declaration. This note confirmed that Britain was in favour of a Jewish homeland being set up in Palestine, but it was carefully worded so as not to commit the British to support the setting up of an independent Jewish state. The reason for the secrecy was that the British did not want to upset the Arabs whose oil resources they also wished to access. Obviously, the Arabs would not support their territory being given away by Britain without their permission.

Britain's generosity with other nations' territory is legendary. It was repeated when Chamberlain signed Czechoslovakia over to Hitler in 1939 and when Churchill handed half of Poland to Russia after the Second World War. (In fairness, Churchill probably had no choice.) There is an anecdote (probably untrue) that after the ceding of Czechoslovakia to Hitler, Hitler asked if he might have Chamberlain's umbrella. Chamberlain was said to reply, 'No sir, that you may not have for the umbrella is mine.'

After the First World War, certain Arab territories, including Palestine, became British protectorates under mandate from the League of Nations. With the rise of Nazism in Germany, many Jews sought to emigrate to Palestine — a tendency resisted by the British. After the Second World War, large numbers managed to enter Palestine and a growing resistance to the British occupation occurred. A significant group involved in the active resistance was known as the 'Stern Gang' named after its leader, Avraham Stern. In today's terminology, this was a terrorist group. Ultimately, in 1948, the British abandoned their mandate and the Zionists declared an independent Jewish state with Chaim Weizmann as its President, and David Ben-Gurion as its Prime Minister. The United States and the Soviet Union rapidly recognised Israel as a sovereign state.

The establishment of the state of Israel was effectively a usurpation of Arab territory without justification. Even Ben-Gurion admitted that, if he were an Arab, he would also object to the formation of the state of Israel. We are told that the state of Israel has a 'right to exist' and a 'right to defend' itself. Does a thief have a right to defend his stolen property against the claims of its rightful owners? This might seem like a simple statement with an equally simple rejoinder. However, there are two quite distinct issues being confused here:

1. The international convention on possession of territory.

   Territorial occupation is unrelated to moral considerations. Historically, the ownership of territory has gone to those who could conquer it militarily and defend it against all comers. Israel has conquered a certain area of the Middle East and is presently able to hold it by military force. In line with historical precedent, that territory belongs to Israel. However, this does not guarantee that the arrangement will remain permanent. If someone later comes along and displaces the Israelis, the territory will become theirs. As Machiavelli quite correctly pointed out, 'There is no court of appeal for Princes'.

2. The concept of justice.

When traditional occupiers of a territory have been displaced, we might regard that territory as stolen and therefore believe that the conquerors have no right to defend themselves. However, as possession requires that the occupier must be able to defend it militarily, it follows that Israel will defend the territory, whether or not it has any moral right to that land. We might not regard this as an ethical approach but that is how it has always been done and it is unlikely to change in the foreseeable future.

The problem we face now is how to justify the existence of the state of Israel. Certainly, we can accept that it would be nice for Jewish people to have a safe haven, but by what right do we donate the territory of other people to them? What did the Arabs do to the Jews to justify loss of their land? Even if we accept that the German holocaust is a justifiable reason for a Jewish homeland, on what logical basis do we punish the Arabs for Nazi war crimes? Why weren't the Jews given a part of Germany as their safe haven seeing it was Germany that did all the damage? Although all western powers love Jewish finance, there was no question of them allowing an autonomous Jewish state to be established within their sphere of influence. But a Jewish state anywhere else is okay.

Since the establishment of Israel, there has been a massive propaganda effort to seek sympathy for the plight of the Jews and to deflect attention from the injustice of the usurpation of Arab territory. Barely a month goes by without some television documentary outlining some Nazi atrocity against Jews. We are repeatedly told that we must be taught the evils of the holocaust so that such a thing may never happen again. The present atrocities of Israel against the Palestinians show that the Jews certainly haven't learned any lessons from the holocaust. And if they haven't learned anything, how can they expect anyone else to do so?

There are a number of facts that expose the hypocrisy of this propaganda:

1. Seeing the atrocities of the Nazis only teaches others how to perform atrocities and probably provides a few ideas that people would otherwise never think of.

2. There has been no decrease in the tendency of racial groups to engage in genocide (Rwanda, Kosovo and even the Jews exterminating Arabs in Jewish controlled POW camps).

3. There has been no decrease in military powers using torture against their foes (Americans in Abu Ghraib and Guantanamo Bay; Serbs in Kosovo).

The repetitive propaganda relating to Nazi atrocities against the Jews has only one purpose — to lend sympathy for the existence of a state that otherwise has no logical or moral legitimacy.

We also see much hype about Nazi war criminals. As previously discussed, the Nuremberg trials had nothing to do with justice, so why are we still chasing Nazis? This has nothing to do with justice but everything to do with propaganda to justify the state of Israel. How can a prosecution, sixty years after the end of the war, when there are few witnesses of any mental capacity remaining, be just? Why are the taxpayers of western countries footing the bill purely to bolster the propaganda needs of Israel?

Prior to the Second World War, most nations admired the attitude of Nazi Germany toward Jews. Even when Jews were obviously being persecuted in Germany, very few nations offered to accept Jewish immigrants. How many European Jews died as a result of this restriction is conjectural, but many who died in concentration camps could have been saved had Britain and the US accepted them as refugees.

The presence of a Jewish state in the Middle East is very useful to the western powers. The presence of Israel maintains a continual friction in Arab territories that limits their ability to unite and act as a Federation. A Federation would allow Arabs to sell their oil for commercial prices rather than for the give-away prices they presently get. The Australian government, for example, gets about the same revenue (in taxation) for oil as the Arab oil producers are paid for their product.

Why is oil so important to us? It keeps our cars and tractors going, but more importantly, it is vital to the armed forces of western powers. How many battle ships, aeroplanes, tanks or military vehicles could function without oil? Without oil, the United States would not be a military super-power. The hypocrisy of the US in pretending that it wants peace in the Middle East, and that it takes an even-handed approach to the Arab–Israeli conflict, beggars the imagination. Anyone who believes that the western powers want peace in the Middle East must surely be on the first-name terms with the tooth fairy.

US aid to Israel is about $5000 million per year. Why would America give such an enormous amount of aid to a first-world country? What does it get in return? Is this simply Christian charity towards a beloved race? History certainly does not support this thesis and I would be surprised if Jews believed it either. The aid to Israel is about one third of America's total foreign aid. Of this aid, about 40% is military without any accountability as to the use of weapons. As long as the US needs oil and remains a super-power, it will supply weapons to Israel, which presently has the third or fourth most powerful military in the world. The US aid to Palestine is about $120 million per year, of which none is military. Thus, aid to Palestine amounts to a little over 4% of the aid given to Israel. Such is the American definition of even-handedness.

The US invariably vetoes any United Nations censure of Israel, no matter how serious and flagrant the Israeli transgression might be. This might help to explain why Israel can thumb its nose at United Nations' resolutions while Arab nations are criticised for not obeying them. Between September 10, 1972 and November 11, 2006, there were forty-one resolutions in the UN Security Council critical of Israel in which the US was the only power voting against those resolutions – thereby having to exercise its power of veto. In each case, the numbers of nations voting for the resolution were between ten and fourteen members.

If and when western nations no longer have a political and economic motive to be in the Middle East, they will leave and consign Israel to its fate. It is unlikely that the Arabs will ever be likely to tolerate a non-Arab military nation in their midst. The Jews, however, have much to offer in return for a guaranteed safe haven.

There are three reasons why Western support for Israel is likely to dissipate over the next few decades:

1. With the upsurge of China as a world power, which is developing an increasing appetite for oil, there is a definite possibility that British and US control of Middle East oil will gradually diminish.

2. The US economy is now a debtor economy. It is likely that the US ability to finance foreign wars (and foreign

armies such as those of Israel) will decrease.

3. With world pressure to decrease reliance on carbon polluting fuels, the need for oil is likely to decrease.

It would seem that Jews should look to this future and begin negotiations with the Arab states if they wish to retain a Jewish homeland in the Middle East. Perhaps they are already doing so.

'Ask me for that which is mine and I will gladly give it to you. But try to take it from me and I will fight to my last breath to stop you.'
Arab proverb

Perhaps if they simply asked for their safe haven, it would be gladly given to them. Historically, the Arabs have always been better friends to the Jews than any western nation. Ethnically, Jews are more closely related to Arabs than they are to Celts. Antagonism to Jews is prevalent in all western countries. Even today, we have synagogues being daubed with Nazi swastikas and innocent Jews, who are simply minding their own business, being beaten up on the streets. On the other hand, the original kibbutzim in Palestine could never have become established without some neighbourly acts from the Arabs. The Israelis and Arabs need to realise that they are both victims of the same global profit machine. How much Arab or Israeli blood is spilt is of no concern to the profiteers. The need for cheap oil is the important thing. Whether it is the Arab, the Jew or the American taxpayer who pays – money is money.

With conflict in the Middle East, the ability of Arab nations to work together is weakened. This suits the western powers that use this weakness to ensure the supply of cheap oil. If the Arab nations co-operated to set a proper market price for the oil, the western economies would be considerably weakened. The support of western powers for dictatorial regimes in the Middle East ensures that the rulers will cooperate to provide cheap oil in return for military protection against their citizens.

In the future, if a regime refuses to cooperate, its fate will be the same as that of Iraq. The pretence that Iraq was invaded to free the country from despotism and give people freedom is laughable. Other western-orientated regimes of the Middle East are at least as despotic as that of Iraq. While Iraq did as it was told, it enjoyed the support of the US without any talk of despotism. Indeed, the US supplied Iraq with all of the deadly weapons and nerve gases to use against its less-malleable citizens when the policies of Iraq and the US were aligned.

What would be the end result if the Israelis aligned themselves with the Arabs?

1. The Israelis would have genuine peace and security. The state of Israel might have to be modified or disappear as such, but this does not necessarily mean that the culture would be damaged in any way.

2. The combination of Israeli business acumen and industrial know-how with Arab resources could produce an industrial complex in the Middle East that would rival, if not exceed, that of the US.

3. The united front against foreign interests would raise the price of oil and funnel more of its real wealth back into the Middle East countries. If they set a commercial price for their oil, the western economies would be, in a word, stuffed. This problem would be exacerbated by less-developed countries such as China now competing for the available resources and forcing up the prices on a supply and demand basis.

4. The US could not continue to dictate terms to the rest of the world. Without cheap oil, the American military could not function. Almost its entire armoury of ships, tanks and planes would be at a standstill without oil.

From the above discussion, it becomes clear why the US military is presently involved in the Middle East and why it needs to continue the conflict between Jews and Arabs while pretending to do otherwise. If the US loses control over Middle East oil, its economy will be done like the proverbial dinner.

Will Israeli defence and belligerence against their Arab neighbours succeed? Israel no longer appears to be invincible to its neighbours. To the outside observer, Israeli aggression is beginning to look more desperate and less effective; it is beginning to look like the last gasps of a dying nation.

One morning the Sun and the North Wind were arguing about who was the more powerful. As they argued, they noticed a traveller passing along the highway below. In order to test who was the more powerful, they agreed that the one who could first make the traveller remove his cloak would be taken to be the winner.

The North Wind went first and began to generate a light breeze with no effect. He increased the force of his blast – but the harder he blew, the tighter the traveller clasped his cloak around himself. Eventually, he could blow no more and invited the Sun to take his turn.

The sun beamed gently down. As the heat of his rays increased, the traveller began to get warmer and loosened his cloak. Eventually, he was so warm that he removed his cloak altogether.

Aesop (620 BC–564 BC)

22 | NUCLEAR WEAPONS

At the end of World War II, the US was the only nuclear power in the world. This status did not last for long. In the latter part of the 1940s, the Soviet Union tested a nuclear device and the atomic genie was out of the bottle. One can understand the rage of the US administration and military against the Rosenbergs, whom they suspected of delivering atomic secrets to the Soviet Union. The US, in one fell swoop, had gone from being absolute ruler of the world to being in danger of total annihilation by its own weapon.

In terms of logic, the countries that have the greatest advantage in possessing nuclear weapons today are small countries. A small country with a nuclear capability would never be attacked by a larger nation because the damage resulting from nuclear retaliation would fall more heavily on the larger nation. Nuclear weapons have become the great military equalisers of the modern world. No matter how large the ground forces of a major nation, that superiority would be annulled by an atomic capacity of a small nation.

Presently, Iran and North Korea are in the process of developing nuclear weapons. There is much outcry, especially from the US, against this. From the point of view of Iran and North Korea, this development is common sense. Neither of these nations could defend themselves against a conventional military attack from the US, and both nations have been clearly threatened with such attack. Because of this threat, both Iran and North Korea would have to be brain dead to sacrifice the only credible defence they possess. No nation that has once surrendered a nuclear capability has later attained one, and no nation with a known nuclear capability has been attacked by the US. One can be quite sure that the US would never have attacked Iraq if it had honestly thought that Iraq really did have an atomic weapon.

Nowadays, a nuclear capacity is virtually useless to the more powerful nations. Nuclear weapons can really only be used in retaliation. If used as a first-strike option, the retaliation would be formidable. The powerful nations are therefore all harbouring white elephants. The nuclear weapons are costly to produce, costly to protect and, at the end of the day, are useless militarily. Of course, they can potentially wreak much destruction but once atom bombs have been dropped on a country, retaliation would be somewhat pointless as the country would now have very little to defend and the victor would have very little to usurp.

Because of its equalising function, small nations do have a purpose in obtaining a nuclear capability, but only to deter large nations from invading them. If we wish to remove nuclear weapons from the Earth, the security of small nations would have to be assured. This would require the reduction of significant military power of the major nations. The US would not countenance this because such a course would lead to massive economic destruction. It needs to be noted that the military power of the US does not reside in its nuclear arsenal. As we have previously seen, this arsenal is useless as an offensive tactic and it costs an arm and a leg to maintain. US military power resides in its troops and associated materials.

Lately, the US has proposed the removal of all nuclear weapons from the Earth. Total removal of nuclear weapons would again allow the US free reign over the small nations without fear of retaliation. (Perhaps now I am being too cynical.) We are led to believe that if Iran does acquire a nuclear bomb, it will use it on Israel. Simple logic, however, makes the assertion laughable. Israel is a 'one-bomb' country (one nuclear bomb would completely destroy it). Of what use would post-nuclear Israel be to Iran, or indeed, to the Arabs whose territory would also be annihilated?

The real reason for the fear has nothing to do with Israel. A nuclear-armed Iran would counter the ability of the US to dictate terms in the Middle East. The fact that the Israelis are prepared to give their lives to defend American Middle East interests shows how desperately dependent they are on US aid to support their state. Threats by the US to use nuclear force against Iran can only be 'hot air', although one should never overestimate the brain-power of any politician. If a nuclear device were exploded over any Middle East oil fields, the entire oil supplies of the region could be contaminated with radiation. Who would want to buy and use radioactive oil? If oil is in short supply today, an attack on Iran would certainly ensure that there is even less tomorrow.

Every known deployment of US military nuclear technology has been, at best, questionable. In 1991, in Gulf War against Iraq, the US employed *depleted uranium* (DU) in its anti-tank missiles. DU is a very heavy and dense metal and it is very effective at piercing armour. As it passes through armour, it reaches very high temperatures (over two thousand degrees centigrade) and some of it vaporises and coats any other substance with which it comes in contact with radioactivity. Although the authorities claimed that its radioactivity was insignificant, they were blatantly lying. Even a decade after the Gulf War, the regions of Iraq in which it was used still show signs of radioactivity, sometimes at dangerous levels. Significant amounts of U^{236} were found in the Iraqi battle fields. This isotope is not naturally occurring but it is a waste product of nuclear reactors. The number of congenital deformities of children in affected areas is three to ten times higher compared to the pre-war numbers. Many western veterans of the war have absorbed dangerous amounts of uranium and are themselves having deformed children. And, having damaged their own soldiers, the western powers do their damnedest to deny those soldiers any compensation for the damage done. There was absolutely no reason to use DU in order to win the war in Iraq. Its use may have been experimental but it was a blatant act of vandalism whose consequences are destined to last for decades and generations.

In Australia, we are invited to believe that North Korea is likely to send a nuclear missile to bomb Sydney. If you ran North Korea and had, maybe, three nuclear missiles, why would you use one on Australia? What military advantage would that give you? Surely, dropping your entire arsenal on the US would be more to your military advantage. No doubt, the Australian government believes that our 30,000-strong Australian army terrifies the North Korean administration. North Korea has one million soldiers on the border with South Korea alone! Is our government serious or delirious? Does it really expect us to believe that 30,000 Australian troops pose a serious threat to a million North Koreans? Does our government really believe we are that dumb? Perhaps we are.

23 | AUSTRALIAN DEFENCE

Our total armed forces could not defend Canberra – even if they wanted to. Any country with a basic army could subdue Australia before breakfast.

Presently (2008), the Australian government spent about $22 billion per year on defence. We buy tanks and ships and fighter planes to protect our beloved country. But how useful would these be if we were actually attacked? Our tanks, planes and ships could only be utilised if used as an adjunct to some larger foreign army. In fact, this country is totally defenceless (we can't even repel 'boat people' efficiently), and the money spent on defence is simply going into the pockets of foreign munition manufacturers. $22 billion of taxpayers' money is simply being hived off every year for absolutely no advantage. We can't help aged pensioners who are living in poverty and sick people unable to get a hospital bed, but we can spend $22 billion per year to kill people in foreign lands? And when we talk of cost, where does the money go? It does not just disappear – it goes into someone's pocket. Guess whose?

Would the US come to our aid in case of invasion?

Not necessarily so. The ANZUS Treaty does not require any signatory to automatically provide armed forces; it only requires that they 'consult together' and that 'it would act to meet the common danger'. If it were in the national interests of the US to assist us—it would come—but US diplomats have repeatedly stated that it would not necessarily do so.

Note the following two Articles of the ANZUS Treaty:

Article III

The parties will consult together whenever in the opinion of any of them the territorial integrity, political independence or security of any of the parties is threatened in the Pacific.

Article IV

Each party recognizes that an armed attack in the Pacific on any of the Parties would be dangerous to its own peace and security and declares that it would act to meet the common danger in accordance with its constitutional processes.

Any such armed attack and all measures taken as a result thereof shall be immediately reported to the Security Council of the United Nations. Such measures shall be terminated when the Security Council has taken the measures necessary to restore and maintain international peace and security.

Make a note of that: the ANZUS Treaty only applies to threats 'in the Pacific'. The last time I checked a map (admittedly before global warming was apparent), Iraq and Afghanistan were *not* in the Pacific. Nor did the attack on the World Trade Center constitute an armed attack. Australian involvement in Iraq and Afghanistan, therefore, does not come within the terms of the ANZUS Treaty. The involvement of Australian troops is therefore unjustified and almost certainly constitutes a war crime.

Australia could only defend itself by guerrilla warfare waged by a citizen militia. Does anyone in Australia have such training? What would you do (apart from crap yourself) if Australia were attacked tomorrow? Don't expect any help from your politicians – they will be on the first plane out.

24 | SOLDIERS AT WAR (AND AFTER)

In order to induce young people to enlist in the armed services and go to war, the rulers glorify it. We have post-war parades and the issuing of medals to those who have gone to war as an encouragement for others to follow. We have politicians crying crocodile tears over the graves of soldiers whom they sent to war to murder and be murdered. Would soldiers continue to fight if they knew the real reasons behind war?

It is unlikely that many soldiers would be recruited by the following advertisement:

'We need to go to war to improve the wealth of Sir Archibald Mogul. Unfortunately, Sir Archibald's son can't join the fighting forces because he has prior engagements at Lord's and Covent Garden.

There will be casualties, of which you may be one – but that is unlikely. Collateral damage is an unfortunate part of war, but if you happen to be killed, your family will get a small pension. The pension, regrettably, has to be small because it will have to come from taxpayers who are notoriously tight-

fisted.

We are hoping the war will not last too long but it must last a reasonable time because profit is proportional to the duration of a war and to the quantity of armaments that have to be replaced.

However, the big plus from your point of view, is that when you return, there will be impressive military parades to which you will be invited. You will thus be able to march with all the other heroes and display the bunch of medals that will be awarded to you for the selfless service you have given to...er... your country.'

So, naturally, the soldier is told that he is fighting for some great moral reason, such as to protect his or her family and countrymen and women against enslavement, or to free some poor oppressed group of people. No explanation is attempted as to why they need to kill many of those poor oppressed people they have gone there to save. It is sad to see decent American servicemen and women when being interviewed about the war in Iraq who really believe they are helping people rather than destroying them. For this reason, soldiers continue to fight and die in the belief that they are creating a better world for others. Indeed they *are* creating a better world for others, but not the others for whom they believe they are creating it.

We have prolific movies depicting the heroism of war. We have such heroes as John Wayne assaulting a battalion of enemy soldiers with nothing but a rifle, and killing them all. (John Wayne had never experienced one second of real military combat in his life, by the way.) The enthusiasm of enlisting and training, and the thrill of the expectation of going to 'fight the Hun' (or whoever the latest mythical monster is) are soon dispelled when the stark realities of battle hit home. And for those who fall on some foreign battlefield? Well, we arrange lovely cemeteries to which posterity can make a pilgrimage and accord to the unseen and unknown bodies the respect that no one gave a toss about while they were alive.

A soldier might think that their government will not expose them to unnecessary risk nor will it order them to battle that is not necessary for the protection of the country. In return for this they are prepared to obey orders without question. Soldiers are prepared to honour their end of the bargain, but they should not hold their breath waiting for the government to honour its side. Where young men and women are prepared to place their lives on the line in order to defend their country, it is an ultimate betrayal to risk their lives in a scurrilous political adventure that affects the safety of Australia not one jot or tittle. But wars have ever been thus.

It is an interesting phenomenon that it is rare for any animal species to go out of its way to kill its own kind. Humans are no different. It is all right to play soldiers with the 'bang, bang, you're dead' scenario, but it is a different thing to actually kill a fellow human being.

In the First World War, soldiers trained by firing at bulls-eye targets. When it was discovered that there were very few bulls-eye-shaped enemy soldiers on a battlefield and that soldiers had a natural aversion to killing fellow humans, the training targets were made more humanoid. But still, the ability for soldiers to miss their human targets remains exceptionally high. American researchers have found that about 90% of shots fired by soldiers in battle go nowhere near their marks. Thank God for automatic weapons.

In 1914, my father enlisted in the Royal Irish Rifles to fight for King and Country (as one did). For many years, he spoke very little about that war. He never attended an ANZAC Day or any other such parade on the basis that such parades only serve to glorify war. Interestingly, many returned servicemen of the First and Second World Wars were of like mind. Our veterans go to ANZAC Day parades to talk to the only people who can understand what they went through and to honour their friends who did not come back.

Those who have experienced the carnage and cruelty of war are usually reticent to talk about it. Perhaps they think that they were alone in understanding its barbarity. They have all, however, learnt that war is not the glorious exercise the rest of us are invited to believe. If those veterans who do march realised that their display of gallantry, born out of loss and suffering, is being used to drum up gun-fodder for the next war, perhaps we would see the end of such parades.

During his later years, my father did discuss his experiences to some extent, but the things that were important to him, and presumably to the other infantrymen, were not the great battles and clever tactics. The battles of Messines or Passchendaele ridges were no more or less important than the Battle of the Somme to him — they all involved artillery bombardments, trenches full of water and mud, continuous days without sleep and the perpetual lice crawling under one's uniform. He did tell of going into the trenches for four days at a stretch, during which one had to be continually alert and awake. If an officer caught a man sleeping, the man would almost certainly be shot. Whenever a dawn assault was planned, the signal to 'go over the top' would be given. An officer would come along the trenches with a pistol and anyone who had not advanced would also be shot. This was not a one-way street, however. Occasionally, an officer would be found with his toes turned up for no discernible reason.

My father also told of his friend standing on the fire-step of the trench and looking over the parapet towards enemy lines. A shot rang out and he was sprayed with his friend's brains. Anyone who believes that such an incident would have no effect on a soldier, have no sense of reality. And our government is contemplating putting women soldiers in the front line? Of course, no woman should be denied any privilege accorded to men.

After four days of constant duty in the trenches, the infantrymen would come back behind the lines for rest and recreation. This would occur at night to avoid enemy bombardment. The British Army, renowned for its discipline, still insisted on soldiers presenting themselves for a parade at 6:00am next morning in full uniform with boots and ammunition in sparkling condition. The soldiers soon learnt to throw their dirty ammunition over the parapets and replace it with new supplies from the ammunition boxes as they came down from the lines in order to save themselves the trouble of cleaning it before the next day's parade.

One particular day, the allied lines were able to advance. On looking beyond the German lines, trains taking coal from France to Germany were observed. This knowledge was dutifully passed back to the British artillery for action. Nothing happened! Later, the soldiers found out that Germany had contracts with the French coal mines; it would not be cricket to damage the property of one's ally! After the indignities of the trenches and seeing comrades die, and now seeing the war effort being promoted for commercial interests, my father and many other soldiers did not fire another shot for the rest of the war. Strangely, the boy who went to France to fight for King and Country came back as 'red' as the backside of a baboon.

Soldiers on either side of any conflict are raw materials for the same profit machine. It is the same industrialists and arms dealers who profit from both sides of the conflict. They remain immune from danger and do not appear to be involved in anything except a patriotic duty. If a soldier is damaged or destroyed, he is easily replaced—and quite cheaply too. Even more cheaply than the missile he fires!

About 25% of soldiers experiencing a battle for the first time, wet their pants. Although, those to whom this happens feel ashamed, it is not a sign of cowardice but a normal physiological reaction to extreme danger. A full bladder is more easily injured than an empty one, and a full bladder is extra weight that one does not need during a 'fight or flight' reaction. Where soldiers experience the death of comrades at close range in battles, many of them develop intense feelings of guilt. The feeling is: 'Why did he die and not me. I don't deserve to be alive.'

Those of us who have never experienced battle cannot appreciate the psychological damage done by war. The continual threat of death leads to recurring nightmares in those who survive. The incidence of suicide and PTSD (Post Traumatic Stress Disorder) in war veterans is extraordinarily high.

Wars are great on television, but the soldier who has to live through its horrors, finds it less enjoyable. We are allowing our best and most patriotic young citizens to be maimed and psychologically destroyed in wars that have no justifiable purpose and no likelihood of victory. But who cares? The battle is over, the profits have been banked. The spent gun-fodder can make its own arrangements.

And what about the loved ones left behind? One of the most poignant descriptions must surely be the final verse of *Abdul Abulbul Amir*, written by Percy French in 1877 for a concert at Trinity College:

> 'A Muscovite maiden her sad vigil keeps
> 'Neath the light of the cold Northern Star
> And the name that she murmurs,
> In vain, as she sleeps
> Is Ivan Petrovski Skivar.'

PART V

POLITICAL MANIPULATION OF
GLOBAL CONCERNS

25 | CLIMATE CHANGE

Significant changes in the world's climate seem to be occurring, especially over the past fifty years. But what precisely are the changes that worry us?

In Australia, the main problem is decreased rainfall and an increased incidence of major fires. Elsewhere, there is the problem of major storms and floods. Let us look at these problems individually and consider possible causation.

Decreased rainfall

Where does the rain come from? Clouds.
Where do the clouds come from? Evaporated water.
Where does the evaporated water come from? Oceans, lakes, rivers, soil-moisture and trees.

Or, to put the process in chronological sequence:

1) Water evaporates into the atmosphere to form clouds.
2) With cooling of the clouds, the moisture condenses and falls as rain.

Because the prevailing winds in Australia are predominantly westerlies, the clouds move eastwards, thus, a decreased rainfall will occur in Eastern regions if there is a decrease of evaporation of water into the atmosphere, or if the atmosphere remains too hot for precipitation to occur. But what happens to the moisture that remains in the atmosphere because the atmosphere is too hot? Clearly, that moisture will be carried further east by the prevailing winds. If a high load of such moisture now cools, floods will result.

So, if we want to increase rainfall, we need to evaporate more water into the atmosphere and ensure cooling where we want the rain to fall. As mentioned above, two of the main sources of atmospheric water are *expanses of water* (oceans, lakes and rivers) and *trees*:

1. Water expanses

The land mass of Australia tends to lack these. But we do have an enormous potential lake – Lake Eyre. This usually dry lake is about fifteen metres below the sea level and has an area of about 9,500km2. If this lake were simply connected to the Southern Ocean by pipeline, it would provide an enormous evaporation basin and thereby increase the rainfall to a large region of central Australia. One farmer from the Western District of Victoria once told me: 'When Lake Eyre is full we always have a good year.'

2. Trees

It is estimated that about two thirds of the rain that falls on continental Australia is a result of transpiration from trees. Since European settlement, large tracts of trees have been removed. It is little wonder then that our rainfall has decreased commensurately.

The standard temperature at the Earth's surface is 15°C, but at 12 km above the surface, it is -57°C. Now, you would think that the temperature closer to the Sun would be higher, wouldn't you? The reason is that the energy from the Sun strikes the Earth's surface and is re-radiated as a longer wavelength form (red, infra-red). This re-radiated energy is trapped by the *greenhouse gases* in the atmosphere and thereby warms it. The atmosphere is heated from below – from the Sun's energy being re-radiated from the surface of the Earth to the lower atmosphere.

The leaves of plants are green because leaves reflect the wavelengths of the Sun's incident energy that they do not use—the green wavelengths—but they absorb the red and infra-red wavelengths, which are the wavelengths responsible for atmospheric heating. Forests would therefore lead to atmospheric cooling. Where the land is denuded, the Sun's radiant energy is not absorbed and used by plants; instead it is re-radiated into the atmosphere. The result is *global warming*. Our problem of climate change is because we have *created deserts*.

One seventh of the land surface of the Earth is covered by deserts; *desert regions* cover 35% of the planet's land surface. Deserts contain no real mechanism to absorb incident solar energy. They therefore act as hot-plates and are therefore enormous sources of atmospheric heating. The energy generated by these hot-plates prevents precipitation of rain and provides the enormous energy required for storms. If we look around the world, the major deserts occupy a band stretching from the northern temperate to the southern temperate regions (between the latitudes of 40° North and 40° South). It is also of note that the most severe cyclones, hurricanes and storms occur in this same geographical band.

We presently have the Sahara and Arabian deserts of North Africa; the Thar Desert of India; the Talamakan and Gobi deserts of China; the Sonora and Mojave Desert of the United States; and the Great Sandy and Simpson Desert of Australia. We are also well on the way to creating two more deserts by burning the rain forests of Indonesia and South America.

The importance of trees

Trees are vital to the ecology of the planet for the following reasons:

1. Trees produce *atmospheric cooling* as their leaves buffer the solar heat and transpire water (which cools by evaporation).

2. Trees *increase rainfall* by using sub-surface water (lowering the water table) and delivering it to the atmosphere. By lowering the water table, land salinity would be alleviated. The rise in water table is due to water that was previously transpired into the atmosphere being now trapped underground. (Hence our present decrease in rainfall.)

3. Trees *absorb carbon dioxide* and convert it to carbohydrates and hydrocarbons. A by-product of this conversion is the *production of Oxygen*, which animals and humans require in order to live. If we bury carbon dioxide, there is a good chance that we will obliterate our own means of life. Therefore, there is a significant downside to sequestration of carbon dioxide, but there is no downside to the planting of trees.

If farmers converted 2% of their bare paddocks to trees, they would increase their pasture productivity by 20%. They would also increase their stock productivity by providing shade and, in that way, decrease heat stress on their stock. If fodder trees were planted to plantation densities, each hectare of trees could produce up to fifty tonnes of stock fodder per year, even without significant rainfall. The effects of farm-tree planting would be apparent to the farmer within two to five years.

Carbon dioxide

There has been much concentration on the greenhouse effects of *carbon dioxide* (CO_2). It has been noted that the level of CO_2 has crept up from its previous stable level of about 280 parts per million by volume (ppmv) over the past 1,000 years, to today's level of about 375 ppmv. This increase in level is said to be the result of *human activity*.

Carbon dioxide is responsible for less than 5% of the greenhouse gas effects in our atmosphere. The other 95% of the greenhouse effects is due to water vapour. Some scientists try to tell us that this miniscule effect of CO_2 is *the cause* of all of our atmospheric problems. They base this assertion on computer modelling they have done. But the output of computer models depends on the information and assumptions fed in; in computer language: GIGO – garbage in, garbage out. The result of computer modelling is simply a guess. If one is being charitable, one might even call it an intelligent guess, but it is a guess nevertheless.

A guess by a scientist is not scientific evidence!

The CO_2 level in the atmosphere depends on a balance between production and usage. If we look at the dynamics of CO_2, we find that some 186 billion tonnes of CO_2 enters the atmosphere each year. Although CO_2 is entering the atmosphere, there is also roughly the same amount leaving due to uptake by plants, the oceans, etc. About 90 billion tonnes of the CO_2 entering the atmosphere comes from natural land sources such as volcanos or geysers, about 90 billion tonnes from marine sources and the last 6 billion tonnes from human activity. Six billion tonnes out of 186 billion amounts to just over 3%; and as CO_2 only amounts to 5% to the global warming effect, it follows that human behaviour contributes just over 3% of the 5% (1.5 parts per 1000) to global warming.

Blaming carbon dioxide for climate change is a classic example of the fallacy of logic called the *post hoc ergo propter hoc* argument (after this, therefore because of this). Simply because two factors appear together does not mean that one is the cause of the other. Because the CO_2 in the atmosphere has increased does not necessarily mean that this has *caused* global warming. Both global warming and the increase in carbon dioxide content of the atmosphere are the *results* of deafforestation—they are not the *causes* of the climate change. A fact in support of this contention is that there has been no global warming for the past 15 years in spite of an 8% increase in atmospheric carbon dioxide.

Let us look at the history of CO_2 in relation to our planet: 500 million years ago, the Earth's atmosphere was estimated to have about twenty times the present level of carbon dioxide and a very little *oxygen*. At 200 million years ago carbon dioxide had dropped to about 5 times the present level, the global temperature was about 7°C higher than at present, and giant fern forests covered the land. As a result of plant metabolism, oxygen(O_2) was produced and its concentration in the atmosphere rose from zero to its present level of about 21%. From then on, animal life began to explode. Dinosaurs existed in profusion from 200 million to 50 million years ago (dinosaurs lived on this earth for about 150 million years). Now, dinosaurs lived on more than a lettuce leaf a day. So what did they live on? They mainly ate plants, and lots of them. And where did the plants come from? You guessed it — from the CO_2

in the atmosphere. So the higher levels of CO_2 actually generated and maintained life on this planet.

Plants today would grow much better with carbon dioxide levels of about 1000 ppmv. The feeling that something must be done urgently to counter global CO_2 is an illogical panic reaction. Our politicians are like the proverbial knight that mounted his horse and raced off in all directions at once. They seem hell-bent on sequestering (burying) carbon dioxide. But have they considered the catastrophes such an act might create? If we got the level down to 50 ppmv, most of our plant life would die through lack of basic metabolic materials and us with them because plant life generates the oxygen we breathe. If human activity is the cause of global warming, wiping out the human race seems a rather extreme way of solving the problem.

We already know what happens when carbon dioxide is sequestered. There are enormous oil and coal deposits in the Earth. Where do you think they came from? They all originated from CO_2, which used to be in the Earth's atmosphere. And when CO_2 was reduced, our planet changed from being one covered with lush vegetation and with enormous diversity of animal life to one that is now dying. And the 'experts' are now telling us to bury more carbon dioxide. Aren't they satisfied with the present rate of demise of this planet?

Our government, accordingly, has not missed a wonderful taxation opportunity. By its own admission, the most that a carbon emissions tax can do is to *decrease the rate of increase* of atmospheric carbon dioxide in 20 years time (perhaps). One good Australian bushfire will pour more carbon dioxide into the atmosphere in one week than industry will emit in one year. What is the government going to do about that? A straight carbon-emission tax will therefore increase government revenue, but it won't result in any tangible benefit. It is simply an opportunity to swindle the taxpayers out of more money on the pretext that they care.

The answer to global warming then is not the sequestration of carbon dioxide, but the mass- planting of forests. This will combat the problems of drought, high atmospheric carbon dioxide and high global temperature. The removal of the Earth's hot plates will also decrease the incidence of violent storms.

Solutions to Australia's environmental problems

Australia has the ideal conditions to engineer its environment: we have the geography, we have the technology and we have the expertise.

Lake Eyre
The area of the evaporating basin could be controlled with the effect that rainfall could also be controlled. It is of note that when Lake Eyre is full, the eastern states have floods; when Lake Eyre is empty, we have drought.

Apart from acting only as an evaporative basin, a properly engineered pipe line could also use tidal power to generate electricity. Turbines could surely harness a potential shift of 9.5 billion metric tons of water in and out of the lake twice each day as a result of a tidal rise and fall of only one metre.

The Great Artesian Basin
This underground water basin lies to the east of Lake Eyre and has an area of about 1.7 million km2, or about one fifth of the surface area of Australia — an area greater than that of France, Germany and Italy combined. The water table varies from one hundred metres to three kilometres below the surface. It is estimated to store between 64 and 900 million mega litres (ML) of water with a recharge rate of about 1000ML per day compared to a present outflow via bores of about 1500ML per day. A constantly filled Lake

Eyre would help to increase the recharge rate of this basin as a result of evaporation and increased rainfall.

Afforestation

Afforestation would be quite feasible because the soil of central Australia is very fertile and lacks only water to enable it to be agriculturally productive. Indeed, there is the possibility of re–creation of tropical rainforests in this area and reinstatement of diverse animal species. We may have to use water from the Great Artesian Basin, desalinate it and pipe it to the young forests initially, but we have the technology to do it. Afforestation should be thoughtfully planned, and that means the planting of the trees which would be nutritive to the soil and to other plants. This means avoiding eucalypts. Eucalypts produce toxins in their leaves that poison the soil for other plants, and the oil they generate is flammable. Eucalypts poison their competition and create the means for raging bushfires. Such fires kill other flora and fauna and destroy property as well as pouring massive amounts of CO_2 into the atmosphere. After bush fires, we plant more eucalypts. We may as well be planting trees that fill the soil with petrol.

Management of the Murray-Darling Basin

Government intervention in the management of the Murray-Darling Basin will not produce one extra drop of water. No matter how well they manage it today, future increase in population and water usage will mean that all the hype about management will end up being a waste of time and money anyway.

26 | OVERPOPULATION

*'The power of population is infinitely greater than
the power in the earth to produce subsistence for man.'*
Thomas Malthus (1766–1834)

In 1798, English clergyman Thomas Malthus published
An Essay on the Principle of Population. Malthus noted
that procreation of all species increases geometrically
whilst the ability to produce food only increases linearly.
On this basis, he predicted that the human population
would eventually exceed its food supply. At any time for
any species, the tendency of the population is to reach
equilibrium. Procreation increases the population, whilst
famine, disease and death decrease it. (The influence of
Malthus on other thinkers is generally unappreciated.
Darwin directly ascribes Malthus's ideas to his
understanding of the mechanisms of 'Natural Selection'.
The line of reasoning of Malthus in respect to effects of
overpopulation is hauntingly familiar when we look at
Keynes's employment multiplier concept.)

In 1800, the estimated world population was about
one billion. By 1920 it had reached two billion, and by the

year 2000 it had reached six billion. Even though science has increased the ability to produce food, an exponential explosion of population will eventually outrun this ability.

If climate change is due to human activity, what is the point of sequestrating carbon dioxide and rationing water if we continue to ignore the root cause of the problem? What are we doing about limiting or decreasing the human population? If one billion people produce 'x' amount of greenhouse gases, is it not likely that six billions will produce at least '6x' amount of greenhouse gases? Does it not follow that any future increase in population will counteract any atmospheric-limiting measures we presently put in place? Clearly, we are headed down a path of destruction of life as we know it on this planet.

People of good will must start to consider the future. The human race cannot continue to multiply without limit. We have already created huge deserts and are presently wiping out the rainforests that provide the oxygen we breathe. We are wiping out animal species and habitat without any thought of the repercussions. The future of this planet demands we stop this destruction.

While our planet is deteriorating due to overpopulation, we have our religious leaders railing against birth control. The reason for the push against birth control has nothing to do with 'right to life'. The real reason for arguing against birth control is all to do with increasing the numbers of soldiers of the cross; it is all to do with increasing the power of the religious rulers. The fact that many women may suffer and many families may live in poverty is a minor consideration when compared to disadvantages that might be suffered by our religious rulers if there were insufficient underlings to service their needs.

We can provide adequate food, shelter and medical care for all people of this world. We choose not to because we live better at the expense of cheap foreign slave-labour.

'The world has more than enough for man's needs but never enough for man's greed.'

Mahatma Ghandi (1869–1948)

The survival of the human race does not require an exponential population explosion. A world population of about one billion is more than enough. In Africa, we are letting famine, disease and genocide progress without hindrance. This is a totally inhumane and unethical way to limit the increase in population and it will not save the rest of us in the long run.

We do not need wars and slaughter to achieve limits — prudent planning and cooperation can do so. But, in order to make a start, we must first realise there are no superior or inferior races on this earth. Perhaps that will only occur when the superior races have been wiped out by the inferior ones.

SUM|MARY

There is only one apparent purpose for our existence and that is procreation. How that was engineered or why, we do not know. That act, however, does not absorb all our waking hours. The remaining time between birth and death needs to be filled with other activities. Whether that time is filled with sport, creativity or simple meditation makes little difference in the scheme of things: we come, spend our short time and pass on. All we can leave behind is our offspring and the benefit of our experience for those who come after us.

From the point of view of any one individual, most of life is but a game. If we are to enjoy that game, we need to occupy life with things that interest us and give us personal fulfilment. We find that we can achieve much more by using the help and cooperation of others. This leads to many individuals taking unfair advantage of their fellow man. As a result, we have a stratified society in which there is a pecking order — the more senior having dominion over lesser mortals. As we were born into such a society, we accept this as the natural order of things and often do not question the right of those above us to dictate how we should live. In my view, such acceptance retards the advancement of civilisation generally. Most people have great talents to give to society, but these talents are suppressed in order to satisfy the requirements of the rulers.

The adversarial nature of society is encouraged by the rulers because it allows them to dictate how others may live and operate. The prime motive of the rulers is to provide for their own welfare, and often as a result, they counter any opposition to their goals. Wars thus provide the double advantage of enriching them while also destroying their enemies.

It is important for us to understand how we are being manipulated into serving the selfish interests of those who oppress us. There is no natural law which sets one person superior to another. Superiority is a bluff imposed by those who can best manipulate their environment to suit their own ends. Rulers only maintain their position by preying on the ignorance and fears of others. The best defence against this tyranny is knowledge and the realisation that fear is only the result of ignorance. Whenever our politicians or clerics tell us something that elicits fear, we must understand that their intention is to manipulate and subjugate us. Why would they be in any better position to defend us from danger than we, ourselves, are? Why should we be afraid simply because they tell us to be? There is a greater likelihood of being struck by lightning than of being hurt by a terrorist.

We all have secret fears and insecurities. These, again, result from ignorance. There is no crime in *being* ignorant. The crime is in staying ignorant.

Each individual has much to enjoy in life and much to contribute to civilisation. Much of this joy and fulfilment is stifled by the selfishness of a few. We would all be much better off if we encouraged all of the talents of all people rather than trying to climb over their injured bodies to get ourselves to the top.

Many of the ills of society are because we promote an adversarial and competitive environment rather than helping each other to greater attainment:

1. How much crime comes from alienating the less fortunate who, surprisingly, feel that they have some rights to a decent life too?

2. How many people become depressed because they feel that they are alone and not quite as good as the rest?

3. How many great ideas are stifled because a few self-interested people censor these ideas and prevent their publication?

There is no need to be afraid of what might be. There is no reason to believe that you are less important or have less to contribute than anyone else. Every person has great individual talents. You may not have the talents that I have (for which you are, no doubt, extremely grateful), but then, I don't have your talents either. Because I lack many of your talents, at times I may wish to avail myself of them – I do this out of pure selfishness. This I openly admit and I make no apology for it.

Even the observation of plants can teach us much. The propagation of plants depends on giving in order to succeed. Many plants have flowers that secrete nectar – nectar attracts birds and bees which transfer pollen to fertilise other flowers. Other plants produce fruits which are consumed by animals or birds. The seeds of these fruits are thus transferred elsewhere to begin life anew. The plants thus give their surplus in order to fulfil their own objectives.

Because I have come to the realisation that I must

give in order to get something back, I therefore contribute what I know in the selfish hope that you will repay me even more generously.

IN|DEX

Geneva Convention, 140, 162-163

global warming, 184, 197, 200-203

globalisation, 127

good and evil, 53-57

    injustice, 53, 74, 172

government, 25, 27-33, 40-43, 45, 47, 50, 70, 74, 77-81, 84, 87, 107-111, 123-131, 134, 139-140, 145-146, 151-158, 159, 162, 168, 170, 174, 182, 183, 189, 191, 201, 203

great depression, 123, 125

greed, 125, 149, 207

greenhouse gases, 197, 199, 206

Gulf War, 45, 138, 181-182

health, 3, 70, 73, 77-78, 100, 107-111, 168

    health insurance Act 1973, 107

    hospital system, 168

    waiting lists, 109

hierarchy, 23

Hitler, 146, 149-154, 170

homosexuality, 15

House of Representatives, 29

inflation. See banks

insurgent, 44, 79, 136, 152

International Law. See War

IRA, 135

Iran, 157, 179-181

Iraq, 42-48, 51, 69, 134-141, 144-147, 160, 165-168, 177, 180-182, 184, 188

Israel, 169-178, 181

Israelis, 172, 176-177, 181

Jewish communities, 169

Jews, 170-178

justice, 50, 54, 83-93, 136, 159-163, 172-173

justice system, 83-93